T0338888

The Life and Death of Objects

Lars Lerup

The Life and Death of Objects

Autobiography of a Design Project

With a Postscript by Scott Colman

Birkhäuser
Basel

Contents

I
1945–1965
Sweden

The Chair and the City

This book is the autobiography of a long design project. Often interrupted for extended periods, the project never leaves me. Even when dormant, it rushes by every time I contemplate the typical apartment plan and its domestic objects. And the project does so intrusively: as a thought, or a shadow of another object—always disloyal. Adamantly it claims not to be furniture, although it may look like it. The history of the project is the domain in which objecthood emerges in time. Closely related are a series of notes on thoughts motivating the project. Since they are so closely bound to my life, the designed objects and their stories are mixed. A diachronic story interrupted by objects. Designed and built—often years later—but spawned by life experiences. The book goes synchronically—cloudlike. Just like the project itself, it is erratic but insistent on being an integral part of my life and the other project on the city, or urbanization as I now think of it.

The disloyal objects, in contrast to the utility that characterizes furniture, project other agencies. Material rather than disciplinary ones. Agencies that question predetermined stations in domestic space—such as the sofa group's position in the living room—and roles in the grammar of the plan. The plan as it is "laid out" in media and in the persistent encounters with *housie houses*, provokes both "tenderness and aggression"—*the cute*, as it was so elegantly captured by Sianne Ngai.[1] Wonderful for the economy, terrible for the environment, bad for the modern family—all rooted in the disastrous way we conceive the things we make. Telling this story is to make a dent in consumerism—the powerful enterprise that drives urbanization. Both by necessity and purpose, I shift the conversation from the global to the local—where it all begins. Here in the book as a story, drawing, image—knowing that everything we make has a butterfly effect. And yes, we are already in the center of a typhoon.

To mark the beginning of this project, I use a black-and-white photograph. Lying on the floor in our living room, I am building an encampment using empty matchstick boxes, wooden blocks, and military figures. It was taken in 1945 by my father, just returned from the Second World War. He never saw action. Standing guard above the artic circle, he spent five years at the Finnish border. I leave it as a mere marker.

Itinerancy

Apart from my father's occasional trips to Denmark, my parents never went abroad. They each moved once, my mother from a coastal city and my father from the southern coast. I moved many times. Why this generational increase in mobility? My own emigration to America is not unique. Småland, the *Landskap* or province where I was born, has been the

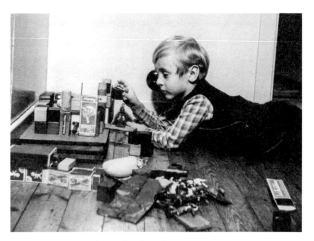

Figure 1. The Author (1945)

source of a steady flow of poor, religious, small-time farmers to America, especially at the end of the nineteenth century and the beginning of the twentieth. My version is not just an emigration, but a series of resettlements—still not unique: America is known for its restlessness. Distances seem shorter here, while at the same time uniquely important. As I have suggested elsewhere, American Distance is a unique, possibly contradictory need to overcome and establish distance—simultaneously. When this steady flux is interrupted, the economy follows suit. There are at least two reasons for moving to America: there are those who come to stake a piece of land and those who come to escape. I belong to the latter kind—the modern kind, the traveling salespeople, who move for a reason and always with the fastest transportation.

For us, it is not a mathematical problem; our ecological footprints are hideously large.

The ease with which each move is made makes me suspicious that the logical purpose is disguised behind an escape secured by an eternal return—the urge to return to the Swedish coast and the regularity with which I find myself there. Despite feeling increasingly removed from Swedish life, I feel closer and closer to its littoral: the zone where the ocean meets the land, where network cities are built. Land's End, where the dream of India (that finds America instead) is born. Littoral, originally *litoralis*, is a generous word used in many ways. For me it is the (tidal) zone where liquid meets solid. The unique zone where movement encounters stasis—a state of steady surprise. Cyclical at best. Standing by its side the back and forth—nature's clock.

Apropos Sleep

Sleeping in the kitchen is an early memory. The bed is a wooden box with a lid. It is a traditional *fållbänk*, a folding bench sat on during the day and slept in at night, although rumor has it that this one housed the pig being fattened for the holidays. Such lore is hard to forget—even more so when you realize that others don't sleep in the kitchen. The box sits under the wide kitchen window. The 1940s are very cold with snow cover often reaching two meters. The black sheet of night sky, lit by millions of stars, fills the window and is separated from me only by double glass. In my horizontal position the city is cut off. At the base inside the double-glazed window a stretch of cotton (while stopping the draft) imitates an eternal winter world. The box, separated by the hissing, waffled generator, hot to the touch, forms, with the window and the sheet of night sky, my own world.

Years later, willed coalitions become tactics to make room for objects.

Green and Blue

The house, with our apartment on the second floor, sits two blocks from the forest in Växsjö, a small administrative town first chartered in 1342. Surrounded by lakes and the Taiga, the world's largest land biome, which expands north and east over Finland and Russia to reappear just across the Atlantic in Canada. Finding the dense coniferous growth oppressive, our three months on the coast in the summer awaken my appetite for the horizon. We rent one room in a typical cross-timbered long house, thirty meters from the harbor. Lerhamn, my father's birthplace, sits on the coast of Öresund. On a clear day we can see Denmark. Aside from the seasonal tourists, everyone is linked to the sea. "Our" house is located at the bottom of a street with seven widows. The husbands all perished at sea. Grandmother's people are all mariners. My father is the first "to go ashore." He goes inland to cultivate the Taiga and, although I must follow, I stay with the coast and all of its associations.

In Lerhamn, the foundation of an aesthetic is formed in the vector between a cigar box and a model boat. The box is found in the strands of algae that appear after the slightest storm; with it comes stuff that floats. In Swedish, the search for flotsam is called *stranda*, derived from the verbs *to beach* or *to run aground*. The most precious is the cedar box, possibly originating in the cigar-smoking Caribbean and carried by the Gulf Stream to our coast. As building materials for model boats, they lead to the slender wooden boat I learn to sail—the *Snipa*, a wooden row and sailboat some four meters long, with a square main sail, triangular foresail, and pointed stern and aft, used for household fishing just off the coast. These boats, an elegant synthesis of craft and wind power, hover as persistent referents to the objects in this book—a shapely hull and tackle that as a combine manifest agency. Everything must move.

Helsingborg

The first city I move to is Helsingborg, thirty kilometers east of Lerhamn. Here I attend engineering school. Despite my disinterest in calculation, the pragmatism sits well with the aesthetics of box and boat. Mr. Christianson, a consummate engineer, hires me—despite my grades. His goal is "building light and thin." That is, he must remove the first form supports under each new concrete slab. The workers refuse. He does so with a knowing smile. (Years later, taking my first flight from Copenhagen Airport, Kastrup, I would notice that you could see through the concrete stairs. The perfect balance between tension and compression.)

I board in a rented room, not labeled a closet since it has a window, but so small that I sit crosswise in bed to work at the desk. A comforting reminder of my kitchen world, now the box is a room.

Two Archipelagos

In the navy, the "house" is reduced to a bunk in a barrack.[2] As demolition divers we play back-up for those who hunt invisible submarines. Russian or American? Still a sore subject. The sleek camouflage-colored navy vessels sit well against the granite of the Baltic archipelago, color from pale pink to pitch gray. This is our world. No cities, only water, islands, and skerries. Some are kept secret from foreign eyes—but not from spies, we are warned. Set ashore by the illusive intruders. Our prey. Years later I would buy a tiny wooden house on one of the islands—the anchor bolts that held our meticulously camouflaged navy boats can still be seen.

Friends bring me to the Eastern Archipelago, north of Göteborg. An encounter in Smögen, thirteen years after leaving the Royal Navy, focuses this autobiography. By sheer luck, objects and littoral are joined—neither leave this story.

When Objects Connect

When meeting land, it is as if the breakers have turned into stone to form a thin, rising and falling land mass. Was this a reaction to the departure of the inland ice or the earlier workings of a restless below? You will never know by looking: here the liquid and the solid are one and the same. Sheltered from a windswept Skagerrak by the land mass, among the thousands of islands and skerries that make up the narrow western archipelago stands a small fishing village. Smögen has been left behind by modern trawling, but is revived by summer guests. Standing at the window in one

Diagram 1. Objects That Connect

of the typical white houses which, with similar others, form a checkerboard pattern on the littoral, I watch as the failing light of afternoon sweeps across the wide outcropping that fills the foreground—beyond and above a whitecapped black sea and an intensely blue sky. Some eight thousand years ago, smooth yet marked, the gray body of petrified rock was last passed over by slowly receding ice; in the narrow valleys, brilliant green swathes of grass are abuzz with bumblebees, grasshoppers, birds, and wasps, all under the watchful eyes of predators—crawling below and laughing above. Small wooden constructions seem haphazardly strewn across the rock surfaces. Suddenly, a tiny figure in a full-length bathrobe enters. Moving slowly across the rock, he or she—hard to say—traverses one of the structures and its purpose becomes clear. But as quickly as the figure disap-

Figure 2. Stair (1972)

pears into a valley, the bridge turns back into an extension of the landscape. What remains will soon fade into darkness. It is already late August, and the rapidly approaching dusk is met by the first autumn storm report brooding over the horizon. The summers in this theater are short but flooded in a relentless light that is so intense, demanding, and invasive that the night is erased—only to return and settle in for months to come.

Never has it been so obvious. Never has what is most familiar seemed so lonely, liberated, and lost to me. Since then, in and out of focus, this early morning drama of earth, weather, and forlorn objects has remained a companion piece for what can only be described as building the unfinished. At first as a visceral, unforgettable experience and later as a laboratory, or a stage for a series of plays. Like a Beckett stage, the site is utterly simple: a wide "pate" of sheer granite bed-rock with an array of isolated human traces. All held in view from a house in a village on the mainland behind, and out there, the raging forecourt to the North Sea. After the first encounter, the stage has served as an anatomical theater of conflict, of doubt, of elation, of sudden lull and wild storms. Yet the strange alienation of physical objects in a grand land-scape has remained. When a tiny human figure appears on the stage, he or she seems a more natural fit than the bridges. In fact, the word *bridge* is deceptive.[3] The drama strips the object of its assigned meaning, pushing it out of reach, onto the stage. And on this stage, the ancient struggle between humankind and nature fades, in place of an internal strug-gle between us and our creations—simultaneously innocent and monstrous.

Hurricanes rage, volcanos erupt, tsunamis inundate. Giant forest fires consume. Glaciers are calving and seas are rising, and we are not just occupants but another geological agency, which, through its interventions—its assemblages of machines—shapes both earth and habitat. Designed things are no longer just means—the avatars of our ingenuity. Instead, there is a slow recognition that designed objects, material and virtual, form a giant swarm that slowly but surely helps destroy its makers' habitat. This realization is paralyzing, so we return to the stage in the archipelago.

Turning away from the window, a square white room dou-bles the exterior world. Walking from this room to the next and through two more, a squared enfilade is completed. It is sparsely furnished, and the familiar objects seem unsure about their place. Even the kitchen assembly seems lost. The same rationale that guides the intimacy of the hull and

Figure 3. Bridges

equipment of fishing boats seems lost without the turbulent sea. Viewed in light of the precise geography of a city apartment, the bisymmetrical four-square plan is startling. The landscape of the city apartment plan has its own landforms; these include sofa groups, dining assemblies, and bedroom arrangements. The guiding generic plan—living, dining, kitchen, bedroom, bathroom— is tattooed on the Western consciousness. The all-too-familiar pieces of furniture always appear in their expected locations. In this prefigured, petrified backdrop, the average middle-class family lives its daily life expecting to find everything in its place—ready to serve. It functions as a global positioning system. Any deviation causes alarm. But not here in the white house. It stands silent on the edge of the sea. The abstract four-leaf clover of identical rooms slows the cultural conspiracy of the Western household. Architecture, now demonstratively separate, has abandoned its role as social determiner. The plan with four identical rooms is here a field of possibility that discards the static, programmed view of order and corresponding devolution of intellectual superiority to communal and personal decisions. In short, it is the opening of a trove of unknown content.

In the fading light of evening, an unexpected symmetry between the rock scene and the four-square appears. The odd presence of the bridges is mirrored in the lost "furniture." Disconcerting at first, it is unexpectedly liberating. It is as if the designed objects (in their all-too-familiar forms) are left to themselves, freed from the iron grip of their masters— freed from obsessive naming and from the shackles of the implied utility fostered by the plan. The fixed and expected are exchanged for the tentative and the ambiguous. Chairs have become objects of unknown capacity. The divorce from the generic plan, where traditionally each piece of furniture is umbilically connected, projects a new condition. Here, the previously distinct purpose of each piece has lost its grip.

Kyrkesund

Forty years later, I stand at the window in another white house, several islands closer to the city. Looking back over Skagerrak, it is impossible not to think of the rising sea. Centuries ago, the receding inland ice poured its meltwater along the valleys of the reshaped rockscape. We were absent then.

Disguised by shifting direction from north to west, the same water is returning. Not for revenge, but as a reminder. Between the sea, the rock, and the white room, a drama has replaced the sleepy walk to the sea. The potential linkages between the oceanographer, the geologist, and the architectural archeologist are yet to be constructed. We, the designers, are left holding a set of white houses with sparse furnishings mirrored by an almost empty rockscape set against an endless sea—an anatomical theater dissected.

With the North Sea's violent western turn my point of view is radically changed. The bridges, no longer haplessly strewn, form a line. Not of defense but of another kind. Abruptly the line is an assemblage—an investigative apparatus turning my work with objects into a laboratory. This is where small things meet the world.

The time-lapse between the encounter with the bridges and the first of the designed objects that follow is at least a decade. The connection between the two events is obscure but possibly motivated by the refusal of the scene to fade away. The discovery of the first visit that reappears time and again is the distance between things, not available in the city. The discrete separations between object and setting made the singularity of each element stand free from the customary assemblages. The distance between the window and the lonely construction sitting on the rock. A distance that is particularly Swedish—a vast country with few occupants. A distance that promotes reflection and highlights separation and difference. A chair just sat on is easily fused with its sitter, while an object in the distance is free from such confusions. The authority of distance is discovered early in forays along the southern coast in search of flotsam—the cedar cigar box that comes with the Gulf Stream. Such distance separates desire and object. Left alone it gains value and independence, heightening the desire-at-a-distance. Since few of the youthful forays ever resulted in a find, objects, all objects, evince a desire not to be found, not to succumb to utility and ownership, to remain always on the lam. It is a desire that takes many forms.

Stockholm

In the fall of 1959, after a bit less than two years on and below the dark seas, the navy puts me ashore on Skeppsholmen in central Stockholm. Just above the jetty, I stumble on Moderna Museet. I enter, having never been to a modern art museum and not realizing that I am about to visit the hottest one in Europe, directed by the legendary Pontus Hultén.

What I encounter is lost in the past, if not mixed with other encounters, since the museum is to remain a regular destination as long as I live in the city; I remember one strange chair that fifteen years later would return with a vengeance.

Bewildered, exalted, I escape along the Skeppsbro to enter *Stan*—slang for Stockholm city—another network city. I recover, since the next day I find my first job as an engineer with the architect Lennart Tham. Breaking tradition, he asks me to design a facade—not the customary role for a technician. Unbeknownst to him, he reawakens the designer. (Photographic evidence shows me building a block *burg* at five.) Tham dies abruptly and Yngve Tegnér, just back from America, buys the office, including the personnel. Most of us stay—he and a partner have won the competition for *Folksamhuset*, a twenty-three-storey office for the insurance company. Tasked with the working drawings for all the stairs, I climb them in my dreams. I live on a sofa in Solna—a suburb. Connected with Stan via the ultra-modern *Tunnelbana* or Metro—the trip to Stan is short. The office is the center of the world—more so in my case since I never seem to leave it. Work is still cast in the architectural culture of Asplund and Lewerentz. Like them, sooner rather than later, you must go south.

Paris

For me it's Paris. Hotel life and the beginning of the unrest. Walasse Ting, the poet who with Sam Francis assembles *1c Life*, lives next door at Hotel de Seine. Known by my nickname Lasse, we laugh that I am the tail of his name. His book is ablaze against the drab grays of the city. As a low-level *gra-teur* (draftsmen are known as "scratchers") chez Raymond Lopez, architecture fades and the city explodes: working to eat, watching rioting with the *flic* swinging his cape weighted with lead; dancing *en ligne* until four in the morning in Le Fiacre; getting to know Buttercup Edwards, Bud Powell's girlfriend living at *La Louisiane* on Rue de Buci—around the corner from my hotel; reading Franz Fanon's *The Wretched of the Earth* (1961); through my childhood friend Gösta I get to know Michel Warren, the painter who lives in Fragonard's old studio; sitting two tables away from James Baldwin signaling his (brief) return to America at Le Flore; "dragging" the boulevards; crowding the Metro with the *clochards* sleeping on the air vents; seeing the general's profile drive by behind a dense human wall lining the Champs Élysées; November 1963, standing stunned at the door of the filled cathedral: "Johnson will be a good president."

A Brief Return

Harald Thafvelin, a friend of Tegnér's, known as the mercurial inventor of a Two-Eyed Perspective—postmodernism *avant la lettre*—writes me, asking me to be his sole draftsman. (In Paris it would be like being an apprentice with Yona Friedman instead of le Corbusier; in America with Bruce Goff instead of Frank Lloyd Wright. In Stockholm it was Peter Celsing.) Since there is an acute housing shortage in Stockholm in the early 1960s, he lets me sleep under a drafting table. Stockholm's answer to the housing shortage is a spread of New Towns, each along the legs of the *Tunnelbana*.

"Hideous, identical concrete contraptions" for Thafvelin and, through the experience of occasionally staying there, to the vagabond-sleeper. My twenty years of "sleeping about" has by now, as the word implies, been embedded.

Murphy's Bed

I'm fine sleeping in bedrooms. But if I wake up, I move. Beds that move, hide in walls, in benches, and in boxes crowd my nocturnal life. Eventually, a strange object has to result. By 2015 it is one of the latest. Beckett is by now a constant voice—stories of entrapment, of death, and comedy appear.

Beckett's Murphy[4] naked, bound to a rocking chair, seeks nothingness in 1938. He sits in a soon to be condemned apartment in West Brompton in London. Coincidentally, a more efficient "Disappearing Bed" already existed in San Francisco. In 1912, William Lawrence Murphy patents In-a-Dor wall-bed, called simply Murphy by its aficionados. In my

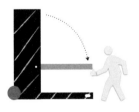

Diagram 2. Objects That Hide

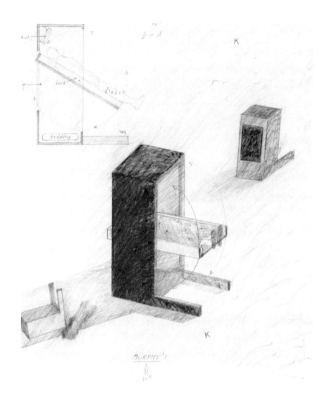

Figure 4. Murphy's Bed

Figure 5. Murphy's Bed (model)

version, the two Murphys form a union—no longer in a wall but in a closet with a bed. For me, our *Murphy's Bed* hints at my mother's rocking chair; two skids at the very long paws of two kangaroos (assistants of Ture Sventon, a childhood detective) and 1950s ice shanties also decked out with skids for easy maneuvering.

And now, still just a model, the pale green wood tower hosts a bed. The movement technology allows the bed to rotate forty-five degrees. Closed, an upstanding box on skis; open, a cantilever dreaming about its sleeper. As one of many freestanding objects in my arsenal, it steps into the everyday. By a simple rotation it tells a "story"—not mine, by the way, but a compressed story of sleep. A nocturnal anecdote.

Fridays

Every Friday, we walk over to *Sturebadet*—a public bath-house. A couple of hours in the sauna (wet and dry) followed by minutes in the ice-cold pool and we disperse. I return to the office. Thafvelin, or Tavve, is just back from the offices of *Blandaren*—a legendary student magazine. Abroad, Swedes are not known for their humor. Tavve, writing and drawing in *Blandaren*, is very funny. Already present, Lennart Lindquist, just returned from years in Mexico. Artist, philanderer, raconteur, he holds court, glass in hand. We are waiting for the model. Once he or she arrives, we draw for hours. The years of drawing models have a direct and decisive effect on the objects.

Although we get to know the models, once in pose they are embodied objects—erect, horizontal, back, front. Standing lit on a low pedestal, the erect shape joins the spare furniture—often I draw both. The step from human bodies in space to inanimate ones is direct. Since then, objects in space are fused with humans in space.

A Note on Space

Space is a contested domain. Gaston Bachelard suggests that we bring "our lairs" with us, making us unresponsive to unfamiliar spaces; the anthropologist Edward Soja seems to agree that space is socially constructed when, in an exploration of urban space, he writes about third space. When Jorge Luis Borges and Michel Serres write, space is obscurely invasive. Borges writes about the "pernicious influences of the metropolis" of Buenos Aires. Serres expands when speculating: "What superstition in the literal sense causes architectural cities to rise above necropoles, gardens above cemeteries, and sculptural works above bodies … everything comes out of death[5] Goethe comes close, when he writes after a visit to Vicenza, Italy:

> *Palladio was a great man … His major problem was that which confronts all modern architects, namely, how to make proper use of columns in domestic architecture, since the combination of columns and walls must always be a contradiction … his creations make us forget that we are hypnotized! There is something divine about his talent, something comparable to the power of a great poet who, out of the worlds of truth and falsehood, creates a third, whose borrowed existence enchants us.*[6]

This *third* space suggests a borrowed existence—space as the furtive play between column and wall. Here, columns are readily replaced by the erect human form. *Objects with Bodies* follow suit. Space is a now a tripartite operation. By implication, objects, particularly when erect, are part and parcel of space. Dependent, they make each other.

Fridays (cont.)

For us three, Friday night is our time, across an inner court in a spacious attic. The courtyard is acoustic. To prove it, Tavve has invented an inhabitant named Arne. We often call him. His answer is the echo. Both Office and *ateljé* are part of a block of buildings slated for demolition. The room is low and generous. Short walls turn to a peaked ceiling. Apart from the brightly lit male model, standing on a short square pedestal, light is low. His pose is a classic lean. The prop is the back of a chair, rather than the customary broken column. Distracting, a black-and-white photograph dangles from the tilted wall/ceiling. It is *Moschophoros*, the *Calf-Bearer*. One of Tavve's obsessions.

Found in 1887 during a dig on the Acropolis in Athens— where architecture begins for Tavve and by osmosis for me— the statue is an erect man carrying a calf on his shoulders, as the Parthenon's columns carry the architrave. Its weight is reflected in the *ekinus,* the slightly flattened pillow, and the *entasis*, the slight convex curve of the column shaft. For us, these are rhetorical manifestations of the considerable weight. For historians, a correction of a visual defect. For Tavve, something much more complex reflected in his binocular *gestalt* perspective.

Magnificent, the *Calf Bearer* now stands in the Acropolis Museum. When found in the *Perserschutt* (roughly, Camp of the Persians), the statue was lying on its back, joining many toppled columns and statues. The two positions, erect and fallen, describe the arc shared by building elements, our likenesses, and us—the lean is one place on that arc. The unavoidable weight of time and material. The lean speaks, albeit not eloquently, about the instability of objects. Explicitly manifested when leaning while being propped up by a scaffold.

In our nightly sessions, the *Calf Bearer* joins us and the model. Tavve and Lennart are both frozen next to me. We are all objects in space. Humans, stone or flesh, leaning against the world. The bearer and the innocent calf as the world. Long gone.

In one of those Friday sessions, I have come back from a visit to Moderna Museet. Probably still laughing, I have just seen Merce Cunningham in *Antic Meet* (1958) with a Thonet chair strapped to his back. I am unsure: was it him in person, or him in a photograph or a print-out? Either way, the encounter seems incredibly important. My elders laugh with me.

That the two years in Tavve's world changed my life is an understatement. Unlike the plan, his way is always searching, always open. I am lucky to have slept under his drawing table.

A Leaning Fireplace

Exactly when the *Leaning Fireplace* appears is clear. Exactly why is not clear. But the Friday figures, burdened and leaning, are suspects. As in the case of *Murphy's Bed*, "strange objects" show up unexpectedly, but on reflection not surprisingly. In another case, an object appears as a direct response to a current event (as is the case here.) Only to later reveal a history. Or as a direct reflection of objects' uncanny capacity to prompt their own stories.

It is late afternoon in November 1989. We are in California. At 5:04 p.m., a horrendous underground thunder accompanying a thrust shifts the vertical gravitational force to a destructive lateral force. The earth's roar stays silent for those who have read about earthquakes. Not for those of us who have been there. We have just been through the Loma Prieta earthquake. The red brick fireplace appearing on both floors in the house reacts. I can hear it buckle behind me as

Diagram 3. Objects That Lean I

I run out of the house. Later I find that its crown fell off. The old wood house probably cried too—an earlier crack in the foundation is wider and the floors slope a bit more.

Mysteriously, I have a painting of a leaning fireplace dated August 1989. Be that as it may, sometime after the earthquake I ask Bill Green to build a model of the painted fireplace. There it sits. No question, this one is a strange object. Leaning out of kilter, it implies that we are in a fix. Somehow all is not well. The fear of falling.

The sudden proliferation of leaning building elements suggests the opposite. The *Leaning Fireplace* seems more problematic than a leaning column. We share the fire. We share the shapeliness. The tower in Pisa is close to the *Leaning Fireplace*, and to us. Columns, unless classical and Greek, are

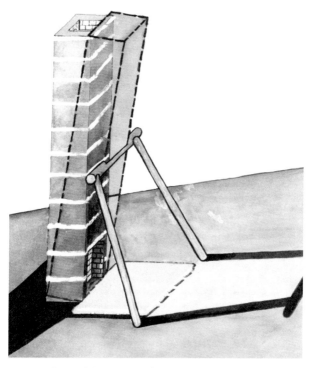

Figure 6. Leaning Fireplace

abstract. To make things lean, aside from the technical questions, now greatly improved by digital calculation, is a multi-faceted provocation. Being sensorial, there is an "aesthetics of leaning." Suddenly, graphically, gravity appears—the pull that the earth has on all of us. Aesthetics, in the Greek sense, has its roots in both the things that we perceive and our ability to perceive. Vision and sense. As with dramatic heights, we *sense* the lean in our bodies—the ancient sympathy we have with the ground below us.

And how about nature's wrath and us, the physical sense of dread and fear that we experience viewing an image of coastal urbanization destroyed by a hurricane? Yet, as an image, there is abhorrent yet seductive beauty in the vulnerability of human constructions. Is this a necessity for all aesthetics? A direct reflection of the way we encounter objects? There is always a side we don't see.[7]

**

Tight-lipped, if not completely mute, the leaning figure pokes us with these insinuations. The result is a vaguely schizophrenic figure, deceptively secured by the overturned wooden U, while the bricks normally held in place by joints of mortar secured by gravity, all in plumb, are now, in the slight lean, a bit vulnerable—the swerve reappears, now to haunt. When, in the aftermath, the balloon-frame house stands unscathed, the elegance of elastic yet stable wood framing is contradicted by the vulnerability of the brick fireplace that must fend for itself. This, in the end, is the prop, a Dali crutch, an aesthetic implement that secures the fireplace.

32

Life in the City

The years in Stockholm have a powerful cumulative effect. Seamlessly, work and life are one. We are all young. Our elders too. Hierarchy is fuzzy, we all believe in architecture—no need for applied discipline. Architecture never leaves the room, office, *bastu*, bar, or apartment. No one has a lease because all apartments are waiting to be demolished. Kitchen, bathroom, furniture—everything is third-hand. "And the plan?" Don't make me laugh. For my comrades this is an escape from home. For me it is evidence. The old *Stenstad* (stone city) is unmoored from the *urberget* (bedrock)—but positively so, since architecture is in the making. Everyone is onboard. The intense camaraderie stands in contrast to the disciplinary bonds of the navy. The family, for those who have one, waits patiently in the background. Time has polished the edges—there must have been some. What's left is a time capsule where the pieces fit—life and work. "A worker's paradise." Its insularity confirmed for me by an abrupt ending—*the new suburbs*.

It takes time before I realize that by working for architects like Tham, Tegnér, and Thafvelin I miss that a powerful bureaucracy is building the New Towns. Saddled with housing an emerging middleclass, Social Democracy's natural partner is the building industry—architects are just bit players. With this realization I begin, very slowly, to understand that architecture's tenuous relation with the forces of urbanization is not just a problem for architects. When rationality and modernization take command, other human needs and desires are suppressed and blocked. The lull that I have been privy to—when Stockholm, just before modernization, lingers in a distinct euphoria. A rapture led by Peter Celsing, even if his colleagues were also envious. Single-handedly, he shows that the same political power that is planning the New Towns can accept a "bit of architecture" in central Stockholm. The result is spectacular. Almost ten years after my time in the capsule, *Riksdagen*, *Kulturhuset*, and *Riksbanken* (the Parliament, the House of Culture, and the Central Bank) are built in the span of five years. The ensemble is an exquisite example of how architecture can orchestrate the stage for a democratic culture. Here in the center of the capital city, vision bests rationality.

Realizing that "working for Tavve" gives me a certain aura (among my friends)—a misconception already noted by Aristotle when he says, and I paraphrase, "never confuse yourself with great men"—ambitiously, I apply to architecture school at KTH. I am soundly rejected. Rumor tells me that it may be because of my association with "you know who." After two years in his office, Thafvelin fires me: "the world is waiting," he says. I emigrate to America.

II
1966–1970
California

Going West

After the mandatory immigration stop at JFK, we fly South. We just miss the opening of Palm Beach International Airport. Yet, via Miami, we end up next door, in West Palm Beach. Joining friends I met in Europe, we plan to buy a sailboat. Never quite convinced about a maritime future, it is a way to soften the landing, a form of return to the known—to boat and beach. The new (tropical) country confuses such attempts.

A couple of weeks later, we "Go West". In a new tax-free German car, we retrace the primal move to California. Taking the Southern route, we find a sleepy America—my 1950s *Field & Stream* America. All too soon, we are abruptly awakened by the Vietnam War. Despite being too old to go to war, I don't fully escape either—my future Berkeley being steeped in the war, while the valley that I pass through still hangs on to field and stream. Here, I get a taste of times past.

Driving in through Needles, we dive into the Central Valley. Already intoxicated by the ride across the continent, we turn right in Fresno and the smell of orange blossom fills the car. Backed by the photo-realism of the Sierras, we land in Three Rivers, California. In view of the instant communications of social media, the way we came to be here seems like magic: a brief encounter with David Green, an American artist, and a scribbled address on a ferry between Marseilles and Palma de Mallorca in 1963. One letter and six years later, we join him at his house. No plan here: we sleep at opposite ends of a mezzanine reached by ladders. Like a shape-shifted Paris restaurant stretched into a long loft, the house clings to the steep hillside. If it had been built in steel and glass rather than redwood, Los Angeles modernism would have noticed.

Extending the long house, we add a studio. Drawn on a piece of plywood, we build it. Bohemia of this type could at that time be found all over the West. The urban version is Haight-Ashbury in San Francisco. We move there in the summer of 1966. The fifties last another month. The guitars in the cafés announce the transition.

English is still a spoken language for me. With no television or daily paper, I am still oblivious to the mounting tensions. Finding work as a draftsman with Claude Oakland, I draw plans of the last generation of Eichler Homes, the legendary houses that break the border between inside and outside. Plans again—although these are good. Instrumental, I am made aware that "our" organization of space is controversial—maybe even radical. As intended by the architects, the Eichler house stands in contrast to the standard suburban house plan: insert an *atrium* in the center of the standard plan and all the usual suspects are rearranged! While the regular plan is universal and fits everywhere, a plan interrupted by an atrium speaks of climate, of specificity, harking back to Spanish California. A way to live with the landscape.

The atrium shows how certain material interventions in an established spatial organization alters its social overwriting—in this case the family narrative. Made possible by the same material agency that upholds the plan. Fixed, frozen, and seemingly unchangeable, the plan is interrupted by the atrium. The family narrative, however, has its own momentum. Slowly, I am beginning to understand that change demands the collusion of both.

To me, it is material proof: we can weaponize design. Unobtrusively so, like a secret handshake between architect and client. Casting but a shadow on the Master Plan. As is made clear to me in this clash, the standard plan is profoundly different from its Swedish version—that manifestation of "the democratic way to raise a family" and emblem of the Swedish Welfare State. The American Master Plan is a cash machine. It has left all such ideological "gush" behind. Here, it is value-free, just business.

The Plan Again

Nota bene, such disruptive strategies must be cognizant of a reality that has little time for such diversions. Simply put, the plan is information. A package of data, shared and distributed by the building industry (today at a global scale), found in the form of the single-family-house and the apartment, always designed according to the same logic—*an assemblage of rooms*, each labeled according to its purpose. The host of a set of analogical codes, constructed by a complex collusion of religion, the family narrative (the text underpinning the American Dream), and importantly, our economic system. A formidable equation that, since it is viral, has no intention of giving up. The Family, the fundamental reason—or, more accurately, the voucher—for the rigid, today unchangeable, physical organization. What I will refer to as *the plan*.

Firmly consolidated after the Second World War and projected as an existential necessity, as a consumable good, animated as a dream come true it spurs a gigantic but erratic building boom that still underpins the economy. In time, the physical organization and the steady change in the social splits them apart, allowing economics to take charge. As a result, while progressively growing in size, *the physical good* stays roughly the same, while the family undergoes dramatic change. The "suburban housewife" is rapidly turning into an insulting myth. The peak of the nation's divorce rate is reached in 1965. At the other end, marriage is losing its hold on the generation—incidentally revealing that capitalism, the central force behind the robustness of the plan, is not dependent on an integrated family. All that's required are labor units paying the mortgage. The plan is no longer the depiction of a social reality, but an independent commodity, a symbolic scaffold for prosperity—the endlessly repeatable logistics of bedrooms, kitchens, and garages. The true social reality of the plan is the people who build it, backed up by the vast apparatus of know-how, facilities, supplies, and capital—in short, the urbanization-industrial complex.

Ironically, the disintegration of the family takes place in the same plan that fosters the traditional family, an invention shaped by the Industrial Revolution. As a new flexible labor unit it is progressively severed from its safety net—the extended family—essential in a highly volatile and flexible economy. The subsequent disintegration of the family reflects the atomization of the labor market. While the privileged live on another planet, all members of the traditional family must "work." Ideally, two are paid, while the under-aged are kept occupied, paid for under the banner of "education." Crudely put, the modern family is a volatile assemblage of labor units, nominally held together by the slight advantage of shared expenses. Children and mortgages. Many such units hold several jobs at the same time, making life in the apartment a form of hot-desking. And as regards children, their "education" is either a juvenile holding pen or, for those who can afford it, a jobs program promising lawyers at birth.

**

Unpacking the relations between the family narrative and the plan is elemental—only a first step in making clear that new assemblages must be invented, not just to find new plans to better meet the needs of flexible social formations, but to crack the hermetic assemblage of the Plan. To meet its responsibilities in the repair of the Anthropocene. The atrium plan is an example of a first step. At least this plan knows that it is in the gentle weathers of California.

A largely forgotten plan has existed since enslaved people began to control the "back of the Large House": a new house, known as the *Shotgun*—a row of rooms connected by doors. Here, everybody meets. Room labeling is virtually fruitless since rooms have to serve many purposes. Probably brought in memory of life and a house in West Africa, it is reconstructed in the New World. The lack of physical anchoring gives the ruthlessly embattled family structure and identity. Once independent, one from the other, the physical and the social will evolve independently. Architecture will relax in its autonomy. The dwellers will construct a social architecture unencumbered "by other people's plans." Future plans have a lot to learn.

Berkeley and Cambridge

Cal is across the Bay. With a roll of Eichler House Plans and a hastily assembled portfolio, I am accepted into the five-year Bachelor of Architecture program. We move to an apartment in Berkeley. Wide-eyed and stunned, even if somewhat experienced after Paris, I watch two years of unrest in Berkeley: reduced to television images, a strangely abstract Vietnam War and a painfully real, rioting city. Escaping its secluded past, architectural education cracks. Human Sciences invade, students drift. The immigrant/engineer discovers the university. Graduating after two years, I am accepted at the GSD at Harvard. Robinson Hall is on go-slow—the term used when workers protest by radically slowing the pace of production. Willo von Moltke, the director of the Urban Design program, tells me my portfolio is the worst he has seen. My spot was ceded to me by the first choice, who decided not to attend. While the natives protest, the foreign students escape to MIT for the end of batch-processing, the birth of the Media Lab, AI, and Marvin Minsky, the author of *The Society of Mind* some twenty years later. Joan (Joanna) Taylor, Walter Isaac's editor, teaches me to write. Jacky Tyrwhitt makes me write and later publish. I redesign Suburbia for my thesis. My friends go to work for Mayor Lindsay in New York City. Berkeley offers me a teaching job. I return to the West Coast.

III
1970–1985
University of California, Berkeley

The University

It is the beginning of fall term, 1970. In the first faculty meeting, I am introduced to William Russ Ellis, a sociologist, the first non-designer (and second African American) hired in the Architecture Department. (Only later do I realize how consequential outside disciplines would be for me personally.) A former track star, he runs into UCLA, "puts the track shoes on the shelf," and never looks back. As newcomers with a common interest, we become fast friends. Russ claims that "only five percent of the environment affects us"; I disagree, but in light of my view of the plan, ninety-five percent pure villainy is awfully attractive. Sixty years later, these long conversations have transfigured into camaraderie. We have one common experience that we will never forget. It still affects us both.

We often take lunch at the Men's Faculty Club, a beautiful redwood lodge built in the teens of the twentieth century in the spirit of the Hillside Club. Its official answer to the question "what is architecture" is "landscape gardening around a couple of rooms," a once quaint-sounding motto—but not any longer—still palpable here in the club, but otherwise forgotten.

One day, our lunch is unusual for me, less so for Russ Ellis. At the daily buffet, Russ is ahead of me. With our trays filled, we walk into the Grand Hall. Long communal tables invite us. Approaching a table with two occupants, Russ points silently, using his tray. Looking up, one of the professors pushes his tray towards Russ, silently assuming that he is there to take it back to the kitchen. Russ smiles and we sit down. At this time, the Bay Area is undergoing profound social change. A sociologist's confrontation with the architectural discipline is just one example. When we talk and text now, the meeting in the club is embedded in our dialogue.

Without an established slot in the curriculum, urban design is an ambition, redlining and zoning are its reality. My understanding of my own hiring as an urban designer is confusing but it does not stop me. Talking about the city as the cradle of architecture gives me a sense of liberty. Architecture is no longer just about itself. Preparing courses is a leap of faith. Arms and mind wildly flailing. My pulpit is a stage. Once (but only once) I threw a piece of chalk at a sleeping student, fifteen, twenty rows back. He yelped—a perfect hit.

My young colleagues seem equally unhinged from the architectural profession. Yet the campus, like a candy store, bubbles with energy and attraction—especially for me, still aroused by my four wild years of "education." Moves from one revolution to the next. All in the midst of three universities: Berkeley, Harvard, and MIT. Each field, left to itself, flaunting its own disciplinary revolutions. Thus prepared, I faced a new university, guards down, in recovery mode.

A marvelous image illustrates. I find it in one of many attempts to make use of *A Thousand Plateaus*. Faded black and white, the image appears on page 414 in my copy. Titled

Holey Space, it is a still from Sergei Eisenstein's first full length film, *Strike* from 1925. Exploiting the silence, Deleuze and Guattari shamelessly suggest that the image "presents a holey space where a disturbing group of people are rising, each emerging from his or her hole as if from a field mined in all directions."[8] For me, it is the Berkeley campus: no longer in a gloomy haze, but in bright California sunlight. And so it will appear, for the next twenty years.

Equally wild, my version of the Holey Space is the loose assemblage of disciplines and professions, each in the process of momentarily escaping its own silo, suddenly fully exposed to those willing to engage. Naively I do, unaware that some silos will be rabbit holes. All of them are hard to digest and I engage in my search for a place in our discipline. The dive is further complicated by an imagined position of weakness, suffering from the misconception that my discipline is in shambles, and a bit masochistic in light of the exploding metropolis surrounding the University in its Holey Space.

While the aftermath of the sixties is taking shape, we can see the clouds but don't know what they bode. (Later we realize that the administrators have replaced the faculty as the guardians of the university.) In the meantime, my foraging resumes. I meet the anthropologist Paul Rabinow, one of the instigators of participant observation. I read (and run into) Michel Foucault. His analysis of Velasquez's *Las Meninas*, seen next to Picasso's, makes it clear that images cannot replace words or vice versa. Herbert Blumer, the Interactionist, gives credence to itinerancy when he states: "when in doubt, go out and look."[9] Norman Jacobson brings political theory to my pictures of Italian hill towns—no longer possible without a scheming *consigliere*. Returning to

43

James Vance, cities and their crisscrossed in-between draw what Jean Gottmann describes as the "irregularly colloidal mixture of rural and suburban landscapes"[10]—an inseparable fusion aroused by the city. Each of the people and their disciplines has a place in Eisenstein's image.

One of my rabbit holes stems from architecture's desperate search for meaning. Despite its long history, anchoring and generously accommodating every manner of human folly, it is suddenly meaningless. An abstract white box with lots of glass. Before we dive, let me say, although this silo lacks the materialism I am blindly searching for, the ride is marvelous.

Through Marc Eli Blanchard, a humanist with exceptional range, I join the semiotics circle—Umberto Eco, Hubert Damisch, Louis Marin, and Michel de Certeau. Eco's cave, presumably the origin of space, is the very bottom of my rabbit hole. But Eco is magnificent. Strangely, much later, I run into him in at least two European cities. Each time, surrounded by a bevy of young students, he calls out: "How's architecture?" Damisch takes to art what architects know: the perspective doesn't tell the whole story of space. The way he gets out of the iron grip of perspective on painting is the cloud. Serving as a "semiotic operator", the cloud facilitates new pictorial space. I am left with the feeling that architectural space is full of such operators—the family and capitalism, to keep the list short. Louis Marin's wonderful reading of Disneyland gives weight to environmental readings of urban space beyond history. Michel de Certeau, the most unassuming of the three, shows the daily rebellion of workers. Constrained by rules and regulations, they "misread" disciplinary space by finding ways not to work while being paid. In the navy, we call it *knipa*—to "pinch" work time from the Man.

Rabbit hole or springboard, a magnificent intellectual landscape emerges, incoherent, wild, and full of lacunas. In the end it is so demanding and insistent on relevance that by hook or by crook my objects must find a place in this landscape—a landscape that occasionally serves as a flotation device. Or is it the life buoy? Not just saving sailors in my navy, or Rauschenberg's goat at the Moderna Museet, but also my projects? My first book, *Building the Unfinished: Architecture and Human Action* (1977), compels me to put the intellectual foraging "into my own words" and construct the first version of a carpet for my *Strange Objects*.

A Strange Bookcase

It must be during this time that the first *Strange Object* is designed and constructed. Although it could have been prompted by the millions of books stored in university libraries, it is the small customary bookcase you find in each

Diagram 4. Strange Object

plan that attracts my attention. Strange objects like pilot fish live off things around me. Simile is the key. The tiny bookcase, holding a dozen books or so, has no predetermined place in the plan. It floats about and you find it almost anywhere. To find its own internal order and stability, its weight, I shift attention from lost subject to found object. The *Strange Bookcase* is crudely constructed on the back porch in an apartment. It is built in engineered wood, commonly known as particle board, the hateful material that makes a heavy thud when we close a modern kitchen cabinet—after it has squeezed your finger. Tapered to shelve books according to size rather than subject; function over content. A small monument to Functionalism. Later, I include the bookcase among a group of objects that act up.

Teaching and Research

After initial stumbling attempts to teach Studio, the lifeblood of architectural education, I am asked to teach *Environmental Design 4: People and Environment*. It is the beginning of fifteen years of teaching and some four thousand students. Lectures are held in Dwinelle Hall, next to Sproul Plaza, Berkeley's reinvention of political space. Here, undisturbed, every spring I propagate my own revolution of space. At the same time, Ellis introduces me to Symbolic Interactionism. I sit in on lectures by Herbert Blumer, one of its major theorists. By now, the *Calf Bearer* as Atlas carrying the broken world on his shoulders, Foucault's oppressed subjects, de Certeau's rebel workers, and Blumer's communicating subjects make up my *dweller*—the subject of my objects.

Compelled by Blumer's mantra, "when in doubt go out and look," I find a situation where dwellers are in acute conflict with the environment: nursing homes on fire. Human escape from conflagration. It leads to several years of sponsored research financed by the National Bureau of Standards. Using graphics, I argue that in order to prevent casualties, we must understand the progress of fires as played out in a burning nursing home. Comic strips prefiguring computer animation. Our conclusion is to improve the education of both staff and patients. The engineers in Washington want a technological fix. Compartmentalization technology instead of teaching programs. Looking back, the spread of fire is uncomfortably close to the current epidemic spreading through modern nursing homes.

Aside from academic work, closely motivated by the pressure to get tenure, I still think of myself as a professional architect. Quickly, I understand that my assaults on the plan do not sit well with clients. The hegemony of capitalism has a grip on all building. Resale secures the duplication of the plan. Houses without kitchens—or garages, for that matter—remain on paper. And then there is the pressure on all young architects to remain in place. Clients like you on call. This does not go well with my itinerancy.

Paper Architecture

It is hard to build for all of us in the Bay Area. Architecture must find other ways to prosper. In 1975, recommended by Sir Peter Cook, Stanley Saitowitz walks into my office. His dazzling Transvaal House outside Johannesburg is already famous. I hire him to work on my drawings. It does not take long before we are colleagues (although he still refers to me as "my teacher"). Another maverick joins us—Mark Mack, from Austria to boot—a nation with considerable architectural legacy on the West Coast. The three of us start *Western Addition*, a spontaneous gathering of designers meeting occasionally in San Francisco. Architecture is suddenly a spectacle. Drawing is an art. William Stout starts a bookstore. Steven Holl comes south from Washington. Before he moves to New York, he establishes *Pamphlet Architecture*. *Batey Mack* inaugurates *New Primitivism*. A shrewd diversion of Postmodernism. Using a dreamy pre-modernism, the firm builds a series of elegant houses and wineries in the Wine Valleys while polemicizing and publishing built examples in the magazine *Archetype*. Holl asks me to contribute to *Pamphlet Architecture* and I begin to work on my second publication: *Villa Prima Facie*. James Monday, a letterpress printer and architecture graduate student, prints the result. With a touch of Gutenberg, a house is printed—unaware, of course, of our modern capability of digitally *printed houses*. It is intended for my friend Frederick Kuh, the legendary owner of the Spaghetti Factory in San Francisco, but Freddie builds another house. My paper house, a series of walls (green, dry, hot, hard, and wet) lined up in enfilade in a glass house (for tomatoes), remains in book form.

IV
1979–1980
New York City

William Stout Books

In 1978, Peter Eisenman scans Stout Books. He finds *Villa Prima Facie: Pamphlet Architecture 3*. Despite being distinctly postmodern, he calls me (revealing his belief that architecture is first and foremost a discipline, not an ideology). A couple of months later I am at The Institute for Architecture and Urban Studies in New York. Eisenman and I teach studio. Finding no words to describe the sensation, I find myself simultaneously at architecture's Grand Central Station and the Royal Court. Eisenman works on the Seminary of Design in Cannaregio West, Venice, Italy. Modernism and Postmodernism tussle. More a playing field than a war zone. Eisenman and Ken Frampton at one end, Tony Vidler the historian in the middle, Diana Agrest and Mario Gandelsonas, sort of, but not quite, at the other end. The magician Rem Koolhaas writes *Delirious New York* down the hall and expels Architecture from its cozy autonomy to join the city—forever. I work on the *Nofamily House*, my first direct assault on the Single Family Home. Everyone is going at full speed. (The Western architecture world has a momentary center, instantly erased when Eisenman turns to practice.)

Introduced to John Hejduk, the dean at Cooper Union, I teach an additional studio with Robert Slutzky—who is, with Peter Eisenman and Peter Cook (at the Architectural Association, London), the best critic I have sat next to. A lecture in Montreal (as a stand-in, first for Ken Frampton then for Tony Vidler) changes my life. Phyllis Lambert attends and acquires many drawings and models.

The Institute is at this time beginning to crack at the seams. With Eisenman leaving the discipline, he attempts to do both at first; but it is soon obvious to everyone asked to take over that Eisenman is the Institute. When he offers me the directorship, some would say in desperation, I decline and return to Berkeley.

Back on the faculty in Berkeley, I realize my transformation. The year at the Institute was the end of a highly unusual era in which the architectural discipline overturned the primary role of practice. That I remain with this reversal of concern is probably hiding in my itinerancy. My colleagues split up: the architects went to practice and the historians went to universities. I am forty years old and about to begin my most productive era, chronologically confusing and hard to parse professionally. A mass of publications is mixed with lecturing, visiting other institutions, and the construction of objects.

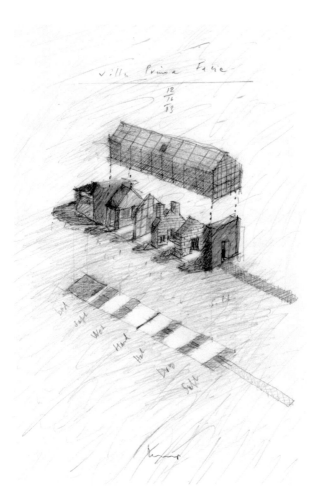

Figure 7. Villa Prima Facie (1983)

V
1980–1985
Berkeley

Rhetoric

The return is fueled by my new comfort with the discipline— the campus is wide open and inviting. A stone's throw from the balcony on Wurster Hall, the College of Environmental Design, is the ancient silo of Rhetoric. I have been led here by my Semiotics friends. How I made a connection between "figures of speech" and martial arts I don't remember. But suddenly "figures of bodily movement" made sense. Late 1970s Russ Ellis and I leave Berkeley and cross the Bay Bridge to go to Chinatown in San Francisco. Here, we attend Master Chang's weekly class of *T'ai chi chuan*. Spread widely apart, a small group of us stand in front of him. Without fanfare, he goes through a series of complex moves— a series of figures acted out by the body—while we watch. Then he asks us to follow him. The body in a fixed position is followed by a sequence of steps involving the entire body, only to return to the fixed position. When "grasping bird's tail" I slow down to put myself in slow motion. While reaching for the bird's tail, I become both body and bird. My mind is left behind. The body takes over to speak, the way face and hands speak in sign language. When "going animal" in a "a stork cooling her tail," the mind is replaced by the body's own agency. I am not sure if I felt or imagined the chi, a desired state of bodily satisfaction.

Looking at these, the body is making space. Each pattern is a ghost space, only apparent when depicted in a video. In rigorous training sessions, the performer attempts to perfect a set of interconnected steps drawn from a series of repeatable, stable, yet elastic figures of form. Without a trace, the body step-by-step draws its own unique ghost-space—the combined results of capacity and constraint. Each an elaboration on the traceless tunnel of lifelong bodily motion—a motion that begins with wiggles and ends with rigor mortis.

The design process is another elaboration of the ghost space. A set of steps performed at the tip of a pencil or electronic pen to become *figures of space*. Unlike the martial art described, design leaves a trace: a house plan reduced to sets of figures (kitchen, bedroom, etc.), in turn burdened with a series of assumptions—this is what you do in kitchens, this is what you do in living rooms, this is what you do in bathrooms, and so on. These behaviorist assumptions are presumptuous, if not absurd.

Let us for a moment liberate design from performance protocols and let architecture speak for itself. Listening to Oscar Niemeyer, while interviewing him in his office overlooking the *balneario* of Copa Cabana in Buenos Aires, gives credibility and weight to his words. In his late nineties, his work still starts with a line drawn on a sheet of paper. He laments that he can no longer draw his much-admired *live-line* in one single sweep. Now, he has to draw the line in a staccato set of short segments, using one hand as a prop of the hand that draws, like a modern tennis backhand stroke.

As in all bodily arts, Niemeyer's physical skill is constrained by age and agility. Designing a house, his thrust of the live-line is the literal escape from the plan. Here, architecture takes charge to free designer and dweller from agendas established by others.

Deviations

Inside the autonomous universe of architectural design, the live-line as agency operates against a fairly stable backdrop of conventions. As a result, we can see Andrew Bromberg's dancing columns as an "intended deviation from ordinary usage"[11] as stipulated by the Classical Orders (an ancient array of columns in sanctioned building styles), in Kowloon Station introduced under the auspices of "architecture for the public,"[12] a domain benefitting from its non-place character. Here, "we're passing through space instead of living in sites and places" (Serres) and are thus somehow freed from established figures of space and form—an acute modernity that architects are effectively utilizing in the design of transitory space.

When we turn to mass housing, such formal liberties are met with resistance from institutional clients. We may see this as a commitment to place-making: the rigidity of being frozen in the obvious absurdities of the standard house plan is presented as a safe zone away from the relentless nomadism of urban life. In fact, this apparent knot of place-making is but another vehicle of this nomadism—and, like all vehicles, a semi-reliable investment opportunity basic to an effective market.

In everyday conversations among the occupants of those frozen plans, deviations from ordinary usage, or *figures of speech*, animate, disrupt, and shape everyday life. Since the deviation from the ordinary could be the mantra of our work with furniture, the conceptual proximity between figures of speech and formal deviations is too intriguing to ignore.

The challenges are obvious from the beginning when we enter this ancient yet unruly art. To illustrate "the intended deviation from ordinary usage,"[13] Arthur Quinn enumerates and explores sixty figures. It soon becomes clear that, despite classification, the art of figures is a complex and theoretically restless one; the internal inertia is considerable, which interferes with meaning and classification. In fact, it is easier to find examples than to truly classify. Take the simple omission of the conjunction—the asyndeton: Quinn cites Montaigne—"I do not understand; I pause; I examine";[14] Shakespeare, in Hamlet—"O! what a noble mind is here o'er-thrown: The courtier's, soldier's, scholar's, eye, tongue, sword";[15] and Caesar himself: "I came, I saw, I conquered."[16] "Here the omission of the conjunctive moves us along," Quinn writes, and just "as an asyndeton can hurry us along, so the polysyndeton [repetition] can slow us down, much like the slow motion of a ceremony."[17] He continues: "In language excess comes in many forms: Accumulatio: "I will not excuse you, you shall not be excus'd; excuses shall not be admitted." Anaphora: "Mad world! Mad kings! Mad composition."[18] Whether the action upon language is an accelerator or decelerator, it feeds off the flow of the narrative; like the small fish that swim next to whales, one cannot live without the other. There appear to be roughly five basic movements: omission, repetition, substitution, arrangement, and effective misspelling. Yet this is just the beginning. There are at least four ways to misspell: "by addition, omission, substitution, or arrangement."[19] Thus, "To reduce Edward to Ed" is to omit part of the name. To change *Ed* to *Ted* is to add to it. To change *Ted* to *Tad* is to substitute. And finally, in changing *God* to *dog*, while displacing a hint of *God* to the verb, as in *doggone*,[20] we have the possibility and complexity in a nutshell.

Turning to deviations in space, such as rotating one chair in order to design a new one, is a technique to slow down, or, better, to interrupt the relentless "transportation"—probably a remnant of place-making—of slowing things down to make us reflect, to stop in front of something that is not part of our errands.

Entering space, we leave the two-dimensional linearity of writing and speech in favor of three-dimensional contortions. Conceptually, such deviations pose a challenge to the development of a spatial rhetoric. While in some situations moves of omission and proliferation will, as in speech, wreak no conceptual havoc, it should come as no surprise that a three-legged stool causes both existential consternation and suspicion, while a five-legged chair may appear silly, bombastic, or—in the case of a swivel office chair—just right. Again, it is clear that both three legs and five slow our sitting since they call stability into question. But this insecurity is rapidly relieved by recognizing the involvement of our own legs. In the dynamic equation of sitting there is always at least one live leg, unless it is missing! Consequently, the rhetorical science of *spatial figures*—a derivative of misspellings—is particularly promising when exploring deviating figures in movement and time. However, as in Quinn's case, it is easier to find examples than to tackle a shifty conceptual domain.

There is no reason to believe that the few moves in the design machine of the *Third Chair* exhaust the potential of mixing the Rietveld or the *Adirondack*. In fact, we can assume that this particular design machine is constrained by the capabilities of the operator and other limitations such as the available technology and materials. Looking over the entire swarm of objects produced under the auspices of the machine reveals a number of similar moves that in turn may add up to an arsenal of moves that is personal and ultimately difficult to enumerate. All the obscure mini-skills that have operated under the horizon since we were building with blocks are seen by the designer as common sense:[21] hidden protocols that have no need to surface since they remain embedded in the designer's agency.

Force Field

In the digital universe, now at the end of an electronic mouse or pen, Niemeyer's work on the live-line has been taken up by a young generation of designers. In Hong Kong's West Kowloon Station, Andrew Bromberg unites a digital live-line with the forces operating in structural systems to produce sets of "dancing columns."[22] The integration of design and physics. In the past, the form of the column came first, with engineering a remedial afterthought. The simultaneity makes the designer an agent of the mysterious operations of quantum mechanics, although this will probably not help us understand why such a modern quasi-object stands up.

(Leaving enough distance between built form and human behavior allows for parallel liberties.) Joining design and structure, we fuse line and force, and we enter a new era of design that gives the live-line its literal meaning.

Scientifically speaking, a chair is a *force field*—a *barrier* of forces which, like a war machine, makes up a stable assemblage that resists the movements and weight of a person. Awakened from its Cinderella sleep, the chair, no longer mute, stands 'electrified' in front of us. The scientific script helps us see the chair as a *dynamic* field of interacting forces in tension and compression. In contradistinction to language as a *full script*, the scientific and design-scripts can be described as *partial scripts*. I do not see an incomplete script as a reduction but as an addition to the object at hand—as a parallel world. An assortment of partial scripts animates an object's reality, even if the actual object is still absent. The chair occupying the same room at the same time, augmented by its force field, hiding some of its sides from our view, is still the reality we stand before. All modern augmentations to the visual still do not erase *the enigmas of an undeniable presence*. This conundrum is what makes us think, bridge, connect, make-sense-of, evolve. We talk, we search, we theorize, we invent, we draw and build. The more we do it, the more real objects become.

Architectural motion studies are a non-existent field, maybe for the same reasons that rhetoric is shifty and best represented by example. We may understand how deviations change language and design, but we have not yet understood what deviations do to us. So, we will return to safer ground without leaving the world of live-lines, the cooling of tails, force fields, and dogs gone.

Diagram 5. Objects That Move

T-Table

Another type of force-field is the table. The plane that both unites and keeps us respectfully apart. Its history is probably as long as our tribal communion. Made in Berkeley in the late eighties, it is a true hybrid—wheels, T-leg, table, handlebars, Masonite, plywood, maple, metal, and rubber wheels. The table meets the wheelbarrow. Kai Gutchow builds the table in the late 1990s. Although not driven by environmental concerns, the entire structure is made of square steel tubes when wood could have been used. From an energy perspective, the joining of materials still suggests that the precise structural selection of materials is a way to minimize non-renewables. The handlebars, borrowed from the wheelbarrow, are made of maple and hinged to return to vertical after use.

A ten-centimeter piece of the wooden handlebar is inserted into the steel tube. The hinged remainders are shaped to be the thinnest where you grab them. An independent steel T is the third leg.

The T-table is produced to serve as a model for a new San Francisco house. Earthquake-prepped, it is encased in an exoskeleton. In an earthquake, the cables would make an instrument, playing when put in tension by the lateral force. Never built, never tested. Instead, it sits quietly on the table in the exhibition accompanied by a text by Richard Rodriguez on the AIDS Crisis.

Sheer neglect left the table in the garden of the studio across from the museum—the bitter end of the Life and Death of Objects. The wet Houston summer sees to that. Its demise still haunts me. How could I have left it in a garden with ninety-five percent humidity and intermittent rain showers?

Dependency

This sense of loss finds an explanation in poetry. The French poet Francis Ponge (1899–1988), whom I discover in 1978 in connection with the writing of *Villa Prima Facie*, speaks up: "The human being is a remarkable body that does not contain its own center of gravity ... it needs an object as a mooring place or counterweight."[23] The house is such a place. But more so when an object leans or moves. Does it become a counterweight? Does it give me balance? Ponge suggests that such a counterweight recalls our touch. Does a shaped bookcase leave me with a thumbprint, when the order of things shifts from subject to object? Clearly objects have become my counterweights—wherever we go the current concern leaves its shadow on both of us.

At mid-decade, the accumulation of ideas, publications, architectural projects and objects seems to go through a catastrophic upswing. I leave my little house on the flats to move into the Berkeley foothills—clearly the other Berkeley, now centered around Chez Panisse and Campus, rather than waiting close to the freeway.

VI
1985–1988
The Last Years in Berkeley

Figure 8. New Zero Interior

Strange Objects

Rails cut across the floor of the interior. Releasing black smoke, a steam engine sits in the center of the image. A table, transfigured with its surface turned ninety degrees to replace two of the four legs. Fixed to a wall, three lighting fixtures made of rain spouts. Three black chairs, looking like

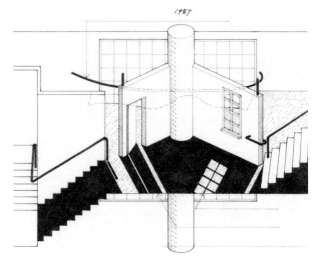

Figure 9. Nofamily House Traps

Mexican *equipales*. A low, angled side table with stubby red legs. This is the central space of New Zero, a late version of Texas Zero, intended for two women in New Orleans. Texas Zero is included in *Planned Assaults*, which Phyllis Lambert publishes in 1987. With a foreword by Lambert and a post-script by Peter Eisenman, the book is splendidly edited by Eve Blau and designed by Eleanor Coponigro.

The text opens with the Nofamily House, armed with traps set for the family narrative: stairs that lead nowhere, redundant doors, liberated handrails, and a Fresh Window.[24] This is followed by a Love House with one half missing and no kitchen. The book closes with Texas Zero, a house (for a divorcée) disguised as a country store. Stocked with a "squad" of objects (in symmetrical formation) rather than canned soup and sides of pork. Arranged around the central axis of an open plan, the squad consists of two leaning fireplaces, a lean-to closet, a last supper table, a which-way chair, a which-way-mirror, and a night-and-day bed. The objects described in the drawing and in New Zero are the first hint at architectonics taking charge of the organization of space. Long in returning from the Classical era, these strange objects burst onto a scene that Bruce Mau suggests needs *Massive Change*. The culmination of decades of preparation.

Wurster Hall

Like all classrooms, Wurster Hall—which house the College of Environmental Design—has an inordinate number of chairs. All are involved in an endless dance. Military squadrons of chairs are turned into circles. Stacked chairs wait. Two facing chairs sitting apart from the educational formations suggest the extracurricular. Students carrying chairs from one room to the next are filling a gap. Yet, while quietly serving their many sitters, the same chairs are largely invisible. Figuratively, this is the chair's momentary death. In the dance, chairs are the focus. We are the objects. Merce Cunningham and the Thonet chair haunt this scene.

Cunningham demonstrates graphically how to interrupt the everyday scene of moving chairs and sitting on them. He selects the legendary Thonet chair—elegant, light, descriptive of its own making. While on the subject of dance-walking, he lifts the chair out of the limited everyday movement patterns. Straps it to his back, as if he is carrying a ghost. And then he dance-walks with a chair as the primary partner. Enraptured, I find myself spinning, not along a creaking black floor but in some space drawn from my memory bank.

Wurster Hall, high on the sloping Berkeley campus, is frequently seen as an architectural offense by non-architects. What they miss in their irritation is the significance of a protruding balcony (strapped to the face of a tower). Just below the top of the grey concrete tower, the cantilevered balcony sticks out. That it does so from the tower of a school centered on the environment is easily missed. Buildings are not radios! But when objects poke at us for no obvious reason, "look at their feet." Where are they going?

In this case the ignored extension *pokes* into the world we ignore. The world seen from the balcony is at this time, in the late 1980s, still glorious, aside from three days in late September when the daily airflow is stopped and the air is filled with the pollution produced in the valley behind it; today, the valley pollution is thickened by burning forests. The topsoil below us feeds the luxurious landscape of the campus. The subsequent decades of the building boom have forced the removal of tons of topsoil—clearly fatal, since its replenishment takes at least ten thousand years. Since the consensus that a Great Acceleration began after 1945, there has been a lingering feeling among ecologists and geologists that we have entered a new geological era, largely the result of human intervention in and on the earth and its resources, many of them non-renewable. Here, the mass production of chairs is one relatively benign example of the acceleration.

Although an unexpected meeting, the dancer's chair and the balcony now poke at us as an ensemble. A Pandora's box, displaying the trees which prosper in the topsoil, the timber milled into sticks and boards, shaved into sheets of plywood, steam-cooked into Masonite. Still holding on to stored carbon. And here the two depart. The concrete of the balcony adds the dark side of all material assemblages: concrete burns lots of carbon. Dancing around, the strapped chair shows that sitting is just a veneer. An unmasking point of view suggests that humans-engaging-chairs are an assemblage with their own peculiar baggage. Embedded dancers are hard to separate from the dance, and so are the chair and the ancient need to sit. Unpacked and seen as an assemblage of both human and machined parts, a new point of view emerges. Once no longer fused under a label, the arrangement of the mechanical, the biological, the economical, and the social becomes explicit. Once it ends up next to us and we allow it to "speak up", we become the objects of its poking. Will it just amuse or irritate, or will it make us aware that we are the object and subject of a contraption that today is more consequential than ever? (Years later, Sanford Kwinter suggests that the way I look at cities is an example of Salvador Dali's paranoid-critical perspective—a perspective probably already in the making at this point.)

In this dance of chairs, the stock chairs found in Wurster Hall will reappear many years later in Berlin where they will leave the ranks of furniture and as objects demonstrate their own peculiar fecundity. At the top of the hierarchy of chairs, they would never be confused with furniture. Especially since its representatives are always found outside the namily narrative and its plan. Chairs have a peculiar status among furniture: they are the only members that are more or less free from the narrative. Free to move about and often found 'out of place' with no alarm. This way they get to meet and form the strangest associations.

Objects That Meet

Revered objects that move about in design circles and are found in publications, museums, and galleries earn their status through persistence over time. Take two famous chairs, Gerrit Rietveld's *Red Blue* chair of 1918–23 and Thomas Lee's *Adirondack* chair of 1903. All chairs have met just by being chairs, but these two meet more intimately and more frequently through a complex mixture of popular demand and curatorial decision. They meet not the way that people do, not because of social arrangement or circumstance, but in kinship. Here with us they meet in affinity—in form and fame. Formally, both are constructed of discrete wooden elements that, when assembled, make distinct figurative constructions. Put side by side and under persistent scrutiny, they appear separated only by degrees, provoking double reading and instability. And only now do both reveal a direct kinship with bridges—networks of wooden elements seemingly held together by will rather than mechanical fasteners and threatening to disassemble and reappear as new figures at any provocation.

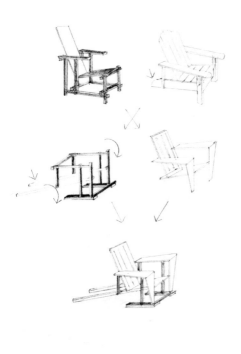

Figure 10. The Invention of the Third Chair

Although the three constructions belong in different worlds (museums, front porches, and landscapes), their elemental closeness brings them together—as if they were originally conceived in the same universe, in a genetic workshop guided by similar biology. Elemental, painted, not quite synthetic, they are in their assembled nature suggestively kinetic—movable, fickle, and inconstant.

Handiness separates such itinerant things from other assemblages such as buildings—cast stiff in lengths, heights, and surfaces. Both the fixed and the peripatetic worlds have their voices, talking among themselves, heard by no one except themselves. Well, that is not quite true; although the voices are embedded—frozen, sure—they can be seen and simultaneously felt. Eyes, hands, and tools know those silent voices well, wandering across legs, backs, seats, and eventually figures. Objects made of a dazzling number of woods, metals, and plastics, many of them memorable, some forgettable. And there are dialects. A Tallboy does not speak Chair, a Sofa does not speak Bed, yet they have carrying and movable corporality in common—the bridge and the bed. This liveliness is of course mere history. Today, *meuble* is just a word in a language,[25] no longer fitting, since such utilitarian things are not in frequent motion but rather frozen-in-place. The dead weight of the well-heeled class. No longer moving—just occasionally moved. The two chairs that meet here do so in defiance of the static, to prompt again the nomadic. To unfreeze the frozen.

Displaced, the human body on the dissection table in the anatomical theater, is replaced by two chairs, both with distinct but similar anatomies. Two stick figures, side by side, stand on the marble slab in my imaginary theatre. The plot is an exercise in aesthetics, in the ancient sense: how one object impinges on another. In this case, it is the aesthetics of "interchairness"—the deliberate engagement of two objects with each other.

On a spectrum of respectability, indeed of class, the first of the two, Gerrit Rietveld's *Red Blue* chair, sits undisputed at the top, while the Lee's *Adirondack* chair occupies a much lower rung—although still a highly respectable position, particularly in the eyes of connoisseurs. Lifted out of this spectrum and off the floor, placed on the imaginary marble slab and put under dissection—under reduction to non-reducible complexity—a wild but democratic thought appears: can we, by using the Disassembler, make a third a chair? Under scrutiny, the chairs speak again. Still just between themselves, but for us to see. Taken apart, the chairs disappear and a narrative is awakened—rudimentary, basic, clumsy, stuttering, yet clear.

The Third Chair

Today, nobody sits on either of the two chairs. The Rietveld is too expensive; the *Adirondack*, a rustic figure, sits abandoned on a porch, bluntly replaced by a softer double in the TV room. The collector donates her Rietveld to the museum while picking up an *Adirondack*—discarded at the other end of town for a recliner—as a showpiece for the never-used veranda. Lateral mobility. The result is a fractured landscape for the *Third Chair*—part front porch, part museum pedestal—a new chance of enhanced potency.

With the two chair corpses dismembered—legs on one side, backs on their backs, armrests and their sides, all in

Figure 11. Third Chair

a neat matrix. A mating game inspired by Fritz Zwicky commences. When dissecting rocket systems, the Swiss-Bulgarian astronomer "invents" (on paper) the German V2 that at the same time is dropped over London. Zwicky later becomes the director of the Pasadena Jet Propulsion Laboratory. He calls the matrix of interchangeable rocket parts a Zwicky Box. The two chairs, dissected into interchangeable parts, similarly serve as a box of possibility. Despite this design machine we are stuck, for weeks on end. In a move of mild exasperation, we return *Red Blue* to its former glory and suddenly a reference to Karl Marx comes to the rescue. He is said to have exclaimed, when encountering his philosophical elder, G. W. F. Hegel: "I found him standing on his head."

In 1917, sixty-five years before, Marcel Duchamp uses rotation to upset the art world. Employing a quarter rotation, he presents a urinal at a Society of Independent Artists exhibition; disconnected from the customary plumbing and flat on its back, the porcelain object sits on a pedestal. Now passing as a sculpture named *Fountain*, signed R. Mutt. In the same year, Duchamp presents a coatrack—also on its back—nailed to the floor at the entry of the Bourgeois Art Gallery in Paris. It is named *Trebuchet*, or *Trap*, alternatively referring to a war machine and a chess move. The robustness of the coat-hanger-on-the wall is shaken—both its use and its placement in the plan—because just as with furniture everything has its place. Lying there on the floor, the hooks are actual fangs, reminiscent of the toothed chains used in road blocks. This is the peculiar quality of many objects that surround us. Find a new assemblage named *Trap*, and you'll be surprised how many willing objects await. The coatrack is particularly effective. Objects shrouded in humor are Duchamp's legacy. In light of the seriousness of his art and our current predicaments, the seemingly effortless humor he and Beckett supply is fundamental in my project. I see my design studio as a theater where all talk at the same time. The resulting bedlam when Deleuze and Guattari's stirrup, Hegel on his head, Duchamp's *Fountain* and *Trebuchet*, and Beckett's *Watt* (appearing just below) bounce back and forth between me and my graduate students—I, for one, am in heaven. And objects, large as a house or small as door handle (Lautréamont's umbrella and sewing machine), all display a new internal liveliness and the very productive ambiguity characteristic of all designed things.

Promptly, we rotate *Red Blue* ninety degrees, without its seat and back leaves. The armrests turn into haunches, while the gridwork of black bars forming the infrastructure remains serviceable. Comically, the heroic device sits upside down—looking for its seat. The pale members of the discombobulated *Adirondack* lie waiting. The dissection has shifted the members from "legs," "seats," and "backs" to "pieces at hand." Inspired by the graphic simplicity of *Red Blue's* black seat and back, we begin to notice the parsimony of the sturdy folk object and progressively see the pieces just as building material. After much design iteration (with legs turning into arms, backs into seats, and vice versa), the *Third Chair* appears like a phoenix. As a synthetic object, both chairs appear inseparable but in parallel. Past purities have disappeared in this fusion, yet the Zwicky Box teases with its promise of other versions of the union of two diverse chairs. This is what happens when we take things apart.

VII
1988–1989
Berlin

The Year before the Fall

1988 is a hectic year. Along with fifteen other American architects, I am invited to participate in the competition for an addition to the Amerika Gedenkbibliothek, the first open-stack library in Germany—a gift from the American people to the West Berliners for their grit during the Berlin Blockade in 1948–49. The jury selects three first-prize winners: Steven Holl, Karen van Lengen, and myself. During two additional rounds over the next year, two of us win; I lose twice. Ultimately the addition is never built—the unification shifts everyone's priorities.

In the 1980s, West Berlin is a cultural pressure tank. Although in the middle of the Cold War, it seems strangely aloof and content behind the Wall. Medieval, the "guild" of architects is wrangling while thriving. The elegant doyen of architecture, Kristin Feireiss of AEDES, sways above it all. She asks me to participate in a large exhibition called *Berlin: Denkmal or Denkmodelle* (monument or model), also in 1988. The choice of subject seems predestined: I am absorbed by the Wall—a wall that in all other modern cities has become the *Ringstrasse*. In the two Berlins, the sharp demarcation of inside and outside is existential—the separation planetary. The Wall is a constant reminder necessarily augmented by an enormous additional military apparatus. Detached while obsessed, I am, like all visitors, not a Berliner. Their view of the Wall is infinitely more complex and harder to discern. Kant might have called it a "good without qualification," while Benjamin would have suggested that it is "viewed under distraction"; Robert Musil would have said that all memorials are with time unseen.[26]

It is in this peculiar abeyance between a public's distinct disinterest and our own obsession that the exhibition *Here the Time Is Always Sunday* is designed. Less explicitly, it is also a turning point for me. My doubts of becoming a practicing architect are confirmed, and a simultaneous crisis of the object surfaces—the sense that everyday objects are foreclosed upon, silenced. It is as if the calisthenics of my earlier objects are too meek, unable to convey the agony of the ancient material culture dramatized by our own deliberate refusal to see them in any other terms than utilitarian. I am beginning to realize that unless set up in a museum, my objects are *unmerklich*, inconspicuous. At the same time, I do not yet appreciate the power of our peripheral recognition; the perception that circulates freely beyond our attention, probably leaving its own peculiar tracks. Instead, I turn to an extreme form of calisthenics.

The Wall

Many urban objects of our history are still with us. The wall (like the tower and the plaza) is such an ancient device. As superstructures, walls defend, offend, retain, and define

Figure 12. The Berlin Wall before the Fall

borders, and when penetrated and outfitted with an opening, they separate but don't divide. As mere lines drawn on a surface, they still harbor many of those agencies, provided the right context exists. But in the case of the Berlin Wall, protective/political gravity supersedes all of these other capacities. The Wall, combined with its guards, supportive technologies, the symbolic significance of a divided nation, and the lore of failed escapes, sits high on the scale of human hostility. As history repeatedly tells us, walls, guards, and supplemental technologies hide in every nation's arsenal of war craft.

To climb this wall with the assistance of a ladder is no great athletic feat, but to tame it as a political contraption takes, as we now know, an astonishing human arsenal of community, political stealth, savvy, and determination. A shrewd union of rationality and chance, worthy of Sheldon Wohlin's reading of Niccolo Machiavelli, in which Wohlin raises him far above the common view of the sinister Renaissance *consiglieri*.[27] Here, Machiavelli's recognition of the need for political actors to have both *virtu* (expertise in the art of politics) and Fortuna[28] (a fickle figure of luck and chance) is brought to the fore.[29] To us, the modern replacements by Frank Chance and Lady Luck, acknowledges that no skills are needed in this quixotic project, just lots of luck: The "undesign" of the Berlin Wall in the grip of the Cold War.

The Anatomical Theater

In 1988 Berlin, we, the designers, are literally and figuratively up against the wall, while the Berliners are divided by an Uncanny Valley.[30] The wall an old, familiar device, here downgraded to a scarecrow—a stick figure in cement-block, topped by half a sewage pipe—hiding a squadron of guards and military hardware. A clumsy rupture, clearly not robotic. Laughable if not so momentous.

A black-and-white photograph of a Berlin street interrupted by the Wall sits on the drafting table. In the distance, three lone pedestrians and an approaching tram head towards the Wall. Once there, the tram must stop, reverse, and return. Boarded-up buildings constitute part of the arsenal of defensive externalities. The photo appears to have been taken from the top of a building in East Berlin. On the other side of the wall, in the far distance, are many more pedestrians and two trams—the visual clash between two political

Figure 13. Objects That Are Thrown (exploration)

systems. Although absolutely still, the trajectories drawn by the two rails point (today) to an inevitable collision.

A second photograph divulges the uncanny obstacle: eloquently demonstrated are the multilayered barriers encountered in the passing from West to East. It's a handbook on the weakness of walls but also a playbook of their 1960s enhancements: symbolically important, the visual presence of the Wall would be useless without its externalities—particularly its "software," the human guards. There are four domains, each outfitted with an arsenal of devices, trebuchets preventing any form of vehicular or armored penetration. In the photograph, a long line of people disappears into a large, anonymous building—a black box hiding the entire political apparatus. A row of individuals spills out at the other end, only to cross two more obstacle courses before finally entering "the free city." A fifth, soft domain is the one-sided military shield of soldiers—the custodians of the death strip—spying from towers and patrolling along the Wall.[31] The concoction of machines and humans and their machinations held in place by a wall—readied for anatomical exploration.

Here the Time Is Always Sunday[32]

It is against this sinister background that we sense the urge for a total suspension of time and space first seen in the still-life of the black-and-white photograph of a militarized valley taken up by all the compensatory externalities backing up the Wall and then in its opposite. In the stark light of the *Realpolitik*, we realize than an architectural solution is ludicrous, but the perfect stage for "the crisis of the object."

With the actual political situation, symbolized by the Wall, as a black-and-white backdrop, the Uncanny Valley becomes our anatomical theater. Both settings respectfully apart. Walter Benjamin's *Berlin Childhood around 1900* is also in the background: his description of the peculiar tranquility that he senses when he enters his grandmother's balcony and looks down in the Hof: here it is always Sunday.[33] The court between the *Vorderhaus* and the *Hinterhaus* sets the tone and pace. The link between *Always Sunday* and Umberto Eco's *open field* is not direct, but as is often the case with design, it readily allows for "strange coalitions." Ecco writes: "The notion of a 'field' is provided by physics and implies a revised vision of the classic relationship poised between cause and effect as a rigid, one-directional system: now a complex interplay of motive forces is envisaged, a configuration of possible events, a complete dynamism of structure. The notion of 'possibility' is a philosophical canon which reflects a widespread tendency in contemporary science; the discard of the static, syllogistic view of order, and corresponding devolution of intellectual authority to personal decision, choice, and social context."[34]

Lobotomy

Geometry has to make itself stone before the word can make itself flesh.
—Michel Serres, *Rome: The Book of Foundations*

With the backstage full, we turn to the action on the stage.[35] Faced with the section of the Wall that as an armless stick figure glares at us, *we split it from head to foot*. Lobotomized, reduced to mere brackets, the wall is cut in two: [-]. While one half stays put, the other is figuratively dragged across the militarized field. A one-hundred-meter-wide no man's land becomes an imaginary Hof. Our Open Field. Benjamin's grandmother's court brought to the scale of the city. As Serres suggests, the lobotomized wall-made-stone-again makes possible a flood of words, flesh: *void, episode, discontinuity, suspension, stoppage, standstill, pause, caesura, recess, rest, break, intermission, interruption, respite, lapse, kangaroo closure, by-work, ornament, supplement, halt, pause, hesitation, rest, recess, breaking-off, bringing to a standstill, cutting the gun, turning off the juice, whoa!, nix!, interlude, hiatus, heterotopia, delay, suspension, hold up, temporization, adjournment, dilly-dallying, a play for time.*

Physics

In this Open Field, a complex interchange of forces operates freely along all three axes, allowing for the arrangement of potential events resulting in an over-all vitality of structure. Unable (and unwilling) to forecast possibilities orchestrated by two opposing political powers, *the material is set free to decide and become.* Although the material is automatically thought of as "buildings," here in our anatomical theater things remain objects. When asked what buildings they are, I shuffle and mutter evasively. (My co-designers answer readily. As students, their drawings and models are always buildings.) Atmospherically, physically and geometrically, the anatomical theater is ready for further action.

The Throw

Finally, a stage on which the shape and materiality of objects can 'decide and become'. But how do we let go of the designer's hand? Michel Serres offers two suggestions. The first is his argument that the game makes us *the attributes* of a soccer ball: here in the anatomical theater, we can choose to be the attributes of the undertakings of objects—of their becoming. The other stems from his *Rome: The Book of Foundations*, in which he sees the stone blocks stacked in buildings as mere weapons arsenals. Serres writes: "We have only ever built to settle the stones, which would otherwise fly continually in our midst." Even more apropos of our task at hand, he continues: "The builder's plans barely count: the architectonic ideal exists only for representation—the point is that projectiles come to rest."[36] Suggestively, we the designers are the attributes of the objects waiting to be thrown.[37]

While looking for suitable objects to throw, we stay with Rome but join Le Corbusier, who suggests that the forms that had been thrown to the Modernist could be found in the primary forms in the Eternal City of Rome. An emblematic drawing charts the ancient objects. Weaponized, but not yet with the right ammunition, Le Corbusier's Roman geometries seem out of the question in Cold War Berlin: the stony rigidity of a pyramid or a sphere has none of the elasticity and spring of a modern urban object. No longer self-contained and geometric, but dynamic and too social ...

Crossing our conversation are the windblown umbrellas found under stoops and in sunken basement entries in cities like New York and Berlin. Jettisoned and deformed, the cheaply constructed umbrellas are turned inside out. Their infrastructure is awkwardly bent while the shield is folded into a wrinkled funnel. The hooked spine is fully exposed, now a mere appendage. The performance is an anatomical self-analysis—the final result of an internal physics of velocity, gravity, and air resistance. And suddenly—out of service—the object-form speaks of itself. Its material personas appear.

The breaking of a thrown object is simultaneously the resistance to total destruction, a material defiance, and an expression of the cooperation between the assemblage and the force of the throw—a *danse macabre* resulting in shape change. By releasing the volcanic powers of the throw on a set of known objects, we get to see the internal strength and weakness of each object—the broken umbrella defies its use but remains familiar despite its near-demise. So, inspired, we go in search of what to throw. In the annals of the modern city, shapes are plentiful. We don't even have to go outside the design studio or the flat world of drawing: here, *Wedges* (parts of wholes or abstracts of stairs) appear, *Zigzags* (as the pre-condition for script), *Bars* (in both senses of the word), and *Cards* (played with at coffee breaks, drawn on, and used for notes and to build remedies for acute edifice envy). And with the fakir beds erased, the objects materialize as multidimensional shapes: thrown and broken by the physics of change, the stage is set.

We have arrived at the state when the very makeup of a thrown morphology, outfitted with structure and surface, suffers the force of its release and crash, revealing the structural makeup hitherto dormant in its original condition—or so is the thought. Our role as designers changes once a form is selected and our skills are applied to the throw:

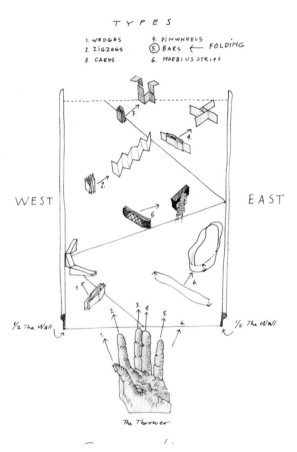

Figure 14. The Throw

we become pitchers with eyes fixed on the projectile that escapes the hand to rush into unforeseen capacities and forms. Architectural baseball, followed by a concern: how much repair?

Missing a physical laboratory, an arsenal of graphic paper figures will have to do. In addition to the zigzag, decks of cards, wedges, pinwheels, bars, and a Möbius strip are selected. Antonio Lao selects the wedge to find a way to scale the wall; in the search for an endless form, Michael Bell selects the Möbius strip; Michael Palmore takes the cards for an elegant game of spatial poker; Tim Rempel throws the pinwheel into a new urban housing type. Bill Green builds a model worthy of a museum; unfortunately, this model later meets its demise in the rushed housecleaning of a storage space at Rice University.

Bar

Of some six thrown objects, the bar is the only one remotely "resulting from a throw." In retrospect, my co-designers are more interested in the object itself than my (not very elaborated) crisis—once thrown, designing the object, rather than expressing material constraints, take over. For me, the task is speculative and unclear. Instinctively, I select three bars, each of various strength and materiality. Once crashed in the Open Field, each bar follows some unwritten material rules, here replaced by an instantly invented aesthetics—"this looks like a designed crash site." Further inspired by J. G. Ballard's *Crash*,[38] and the aforementioned collapsed umbrella, three bars (open, closed and both) begin their

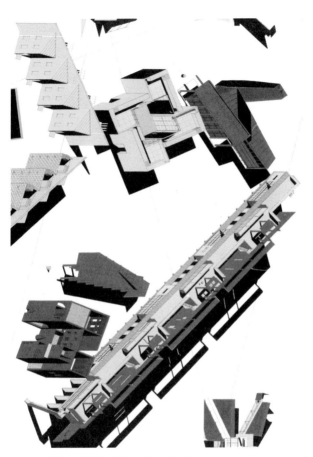

Figure 15. The Throw Completed

Figure 16. Bars

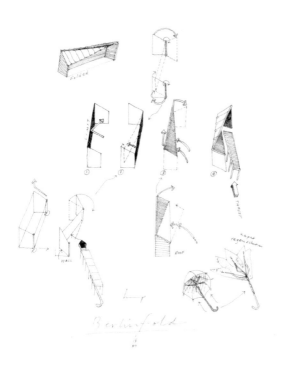

Figure 17. Berlinfold

Figure 18. Thrown Objects

unfolding. Once at rest, the bars—now inexplicably three—
are horizontal, vertical, warped, and intertwined. Just before
the bars are thrown and hit the ground, gravity is zero, but
the inertia of the throw is not zero until the interiors of the
bars come to rest. The force of the throw has then rushed
through the bars the way the lateral force of an earthquake
moves through a building. The thrust of the throw penetrates
each bar and deconstructs it. In the bar building, unlike the
other widgets, the force is such that it sets a bar's degrees
of freedom in motion: columns serve as rotational axes,
plates are folded along their weakest connections, internal
structures are revealed as surfaces that are literally shaken
off. Using its own physics, the object expresses its internal
makeup, its strengths and weaknesses. At rest, it has remade

itself. Collapsed, the gadget opens itself to reveal a hidden interiority—but have we come closer to understanding the truism that we impact the object, and the object impacts us? Does this impact on us just confirm that the more we know about objects the more withdrawn they are? Eternally mysterious, objects are literally out of our hands, especially when we have just thrown them.

Undeniably productive and intriguing, these textual simulations make clear that the crisis is ours, not the objects'. Objects are not (yet) on their own to decide and become. They remain forced into servitude, because we choose to only see them when they are useful. Which in turn has led to the disastrous neglect of their materiality—of their hidden powers. There is some escape in *The Open Work*, where Umberto Eco argues that in its aesthetic formation, a successful work of art ought to display "controlled disorder," and the "the organic fusion of multiple elements."[39] (Eco would publish his book a year after our Berlin intervention, at the same time as the "opening" of the wall. Coincidences of this kind are beautiful in themselves.) In "The Form of Disorder," he suggests that *controlled* disorder is the designer's desire to have some effect on chance.[40] Our Happy Valley is a case study. Here in our open field between the brackets of a split wall, one might hope that objects have truly left the hands of the designer. But this is not the case. A potential only partially fulfilled, the limits of an enactment, the bars are, in the end, domesticated—returned to some form of order. In short, designed. A flat field, graced by objects, equally produced by objects and designers, is obliquely different from both a Happy Valley with its "controlled disorder" and the Uncanny Valley with its "fusion" of humans and machines.

Figure 19. Thrown Objects (perspective)

Here, all objects are facsimiles of humans and their qualities. With their uncanny familiarity, they leave unease in their path. The open work we aspire to ends up, warts and all, still far away, below the horizon. The subsequent ideological shift from East to West seals it, leaving in its wake but scraps of wall, draped in mythology.

Despite the loss of the competition for the library and the realization that the competition and the exhibition were just a product and a respite from the Cold War, the two projects brought together a group of the sort of aficionados that the architectural studio culture spawns. Unforgettable and irreplaceable.

Briefly in Berlin visiting Aedes Gallery at Spreebogen, it is the beginning of my fortieth decade. It is sealed one dark and misty evening: walking along Stromstrasse towards Turmstrasse, Bruno Ganz walks out of the midst, and suddenly I'm cast in *Wings of Desire*—desire being the central motif of the work.

**

Restlessness Again

The complete Peter Wilson (architect, artist, writer, teacher) invites me to teach with him at the AA in London. With a bar at its center, the AA is magical; everyone is hot-desking, and not the least because of its Director Alvin Boyarsky—the architect as impresario. (Again, the functionalist plans, now for modern architecture schools, look hopelessly lost.) The atmospherics dominate the creaking, cramped insides of the black terrace house, on its privileged square. Peter Cook, Koolhaas again, Zaha Hadid, all stoke the pressure cooker. Crammed with a highly energized multitude of designers, probably only possible in a world city. Feeling decentered, not yet realizing that my contrarian position is comfortably at home in hotbeds like the AA, and later at SCI-Arc.[41] It is, in retrospect, the preparation for leaving my alma mater. A separation—put simplistically as the separation between mind and hand—that has never been comfortable, and most certainly never absolute.

In Berkeley, two projects have been shaped: cities and objects—writing and making. I have been teaching Environmental Design 4: People and Environment for fifteen years. I have seen some four thousand students come and go. Objects, the apparent carriers of my wavering between academia and profession, have gone native. Recognized as a fork in my road, the university path is Urbanism; the other path, not until now given a proper place in my work: close to my id, the desire to build, already apparent at age five, is now given exposure. The magnificent James Prestini had taken me out of the studio to the shop. In cahoots with graduate students, the making of objects is an everyday activity.

While the older faculty members argue, the drift towards Super Functionalism is palpable—every emotion must have an expression in form. I remain unconvinced. For me, the built and constructed are already free agents. My ideal plan has already taken shelter in Tafuri's uselessness. My itinerancy acts up; SCI-Arc in Los Angeles invites me as a guest. As a materialist workshop it is a tour de force. Wolf Prix and I teach a studio where all buildings must move. *Objects That Walk*. Robert Mangurian, Thom Mayne, Michael Rotondi, Craig Hodgetts, and Erik Moss are explosive. I write a piece on Frank Gehry, arguing that this is Architecture and cannot be dismissed as art. Progressively, I feel distant from Berkeley's architecture school. With the Holey Space in my luggage, my leave is the opposite of parental. Rotondi asks me to be the Educational Director at SCI-Arc's antenna in Vico Morcote, Switzerland. I accept and take a leave from Berkeley: as fate has it, never to return to its faculty.

VIII
1991–1993
Vico Morcote

Xerox PARC

Just before leaving the Bay Area, I am invited to Xerox PARC by John Seely Brown to redesign his office. But not the usual way: it has to be done in cooperation with two other designers, whom I will not meet until we are finished. Each of us sits in a separate room at the PARC. On the desk is a computer and a wide screen, attended to by several handlers. A jumble of cables connects the computer to an intranet. Unknowingly, we are testing a new way to design. Slow, cumbersome, often interrupted, I use tracing paper on the screen image to adjust a design. One of the handlers delivers it to my partners by hand and foot. In retrospect, we were all witness to a revolution. Now, each of these steps has its own history, its own heroes. With the revolution in mind, I go to SCI-Arc Vico. And productively also back in time.

Vico

There is a small architecture school in Vico Morcote, a tiny mountain village uphill and west of Lugano, Switzerland. On loan from UC Berkeley, I am hired by Sci-Arc to run the teaching program. Its Director, Martin Wagner, is an acquaintance from my days in Zurich; the school is housed in a villa he redesigned. Perfect for my educational dream: *the endless seminar*. Here, students sleep, work and eat. I live a short car ride away. Looking back it is, among many great teaching experiences, the best—not least because of the students, many of them now doing important work: Keith Krumwiede is director of a school in San Francisco; Jennifer Siegal is an ingenious prefab designer in Los Angeles; Andrew Bromberg is design director of a large firm in Hong Kong; Robert Adams is a professor in Ann Harbor whose students' work would make even the best Rube Goldbergs pale.

Wagner is a very good architect. His work is found all over Ticino. I join him in his studio in nearby Carona. For two years, I am an architect. Competition entries, a string of row houses later completed include a Mulino—a water-powered mill found as a ruin, now a grand villa—with its own brook. A series of independent house projects. None are built but remain as paper architecture stuck precariously to the hillside or dangling over the Lago.

My strange objects remain on paper and very much in mind. My son and I draw and paint them incessantly. I visit many of Wagner's projects where he is refurbishing and adding to old houses. Suffering from no plan, the old farm houses make a clear distinction between the building and the household equipment. Houses exist in a *longue durée*. Serving one generation after another, they seem timeless. Tenancy is relatively short. The separation between the built and its inhabitants is graphic, best seen in building-like armoires sitting in splendid isolation. These ambulant bodies have their own lifespan. Staying on to serve the next generation, or leaving to another house. Never quite fixed. The armoires are so prominent and appealing to me that they join my virtual luggage, already crowded by Duchamp's Readymades and Joseph Beuys *Fat Chair* of 1964—another time piece carrying its lifespan on its sleeve. Here, a wedge of solid fat "sits" on an everyday kitchen chair. A simple temperature change will show the difference between substance and object—between life (reduced to fat) and the chair that holds it. *Object with Bodies* are born.

In Ticino, we live in a bubble: an exceptional density of conversation; the compactness of the villages; the independence and seclusion of Ticino culture in an already tiny country. Pipo, who with his brother makes all our steel windows, introduces me to café-correto-grappa and long lunches. Gianni, a former Ferrari race driver, supplies all the woodwork; rides in his Testarossa scare and excite. Wagner is building houses of stone, here to last. All this contributes to something not quite real but more like a living anecdote. A narrative with a distinct beginning and end. Here, architecture reappears, the way it was *lived* in my years in Stockholm. Now, on this ancient southern incline between an Alp and the Po Valley, all distances between design, building, and living are erased. I also know that such legends are just lived and told by sailors and vagabonds.

Objects with Bodies (and Shadows)

With easy access to the Po Valley, Palladio becomes real. Eisenman and I had used the villas in our studios at the Institute a decade earlier. Lived space is far from drawn space.

One makes sound, the other leaves marks on paper and patterns in the mind. Goethe's *Italienische Reise* from 1786 proves a more suitable guide than Colin Rowe's "Mathematics of the Ideal Villa" of 1947. The Institute's A, B, and C spaces fade as I walk into Villa Valmarana (Lisiera) close to Vicenza. If truth be told, space is probably the most enigmatic aspect of our discipline. We all struggle with its conception. Being there makes for a deafening quiet. But not for Goethe, his space is a *third*—Palladio's furtive play between the column and the wall. Columns are often confused with the erect human form, while the abstract wall, despite the human marks of a window or a door, retains its otherness. Elegantly hinting at the human-as-column, Goethe writes that space is not possible without us. Space is always somewhere between us and the built. A mirage that is (as far as we know) only open to us and other animals around. Such ephemeral in-betweens are what architecture aspires too: a tangle of perception (aesthetics), culture, and geometry. Expanding the speculations of this elusive subject, we will turn to other spaces rarely spoken of in buildings and (excluding Bachelard) never in furniture.

Goethe's third has today a fourth dimension. His space is a significant emptiness, ours is filled with effluence. Space is no longer abstract but ever-present, literally tasty—opening another chapter of this evasive subject.

Hiding between the public and the private, or between the private and the very private, such pockets of space, known as *poché*,[42] are usually surmised from reading or the "walking of plans," but are either inaccessible or are accessible only to the initiated. *Poché* is used to give shape to ceremonial space (such as the central Sala in Villa Rotonda. This pocket of material differentiation between the circular and the rectangular may also operate as the load-bearing structure, allowing for multi-story construction. The French *hôtel* or apartment building may be the emblem of this architectural *double entendre*, used by Baron Haussmann as the inhabited facade of the new nineteenth-century Paris, housing the gentrifiers while hiding the poor and restless. The *poché* is used as a filler to make the space it encloses as shapely as possible. Ignored, it becomes new space for us sequestered in the Swiss Villa, where such left-over space is fully occupied, with tiny rooms, embedded beds, storage, studies.

In contemporary apartments, such spatial sophistication is abandoned in favor of regular walls as room separations, and doors as openings. Here, since both structure and domestic servitude have changed dramatically, those past pockets of space, hiding structure or hidden passages used by servants, have reverted to storage. However, the astonishing demand for storage has necessitated plans to include separate rooms for it, and further expansion in the form of furniture: wardrobes, drawers, and chests. Prized by apartment dwellers, fixed and movable storage is spatially ambiguous, inserted between or added to the public/private domain—a suspended nonspace best not seen, hiding anything from food to secrets (the most private of the personal).

As a shadow of the ruminations around space, the objects go on an excursion. The result is some fifty drawings, often done with my four-year-old son. *Shadow* is the keyword here. He occasionally shadows my drawing, while I shadow previously designed objects. Space leaves its thumbprints on us. Both in the Vico Design Studio and in our drawings, the thumbprint takes form. Imagined as objects in felt (Beuys), operating as tightfitting suits for armoires. One specific drawing is probably the embryo of *Blu* (presented in the last chapter): here, a tapered object, with a large square opening at its back, tilts, while being lifted-off the floor and supported by one solitary leg. Salmon-colored with one side in roughed-up plywood. Another set of drawings shows storage objects to fit under sofas and tables: these *Tucks* hold bottles, pipes, and tobacco—sort-of-hidden. Others fit under office tables, rendering the tables useless. This cadre of objects are intruders: often mere shadows, others distinct obstacles. The first-generation objects remain respectable. Accepted in regular furniture categories, even if uncomfortably so. The intruders are out of bounds. Two tactics: fit-in but not quite and intrude; get in the way, make a spectacle.

Closets get socks. Sofas hide the tucks. Negative space is materialized, impossible to inhabit because solid. In our drawings, the thumbprints remain incomplete, hesitant. Beautifully useless. Out of many thumbprints, there is one union of our shadow work and the armoires I see on my tours of Villas. My excursions in the lower Alps, on foot and on paper, tilt my work in a new direction. The suggestion that the *mucche* gracing the hill have one pair of legs shorter than the other pair is met by my son's skepticism. The joke aside, the tilted territory with its majestic farm houses and giant armoires form a double-space. Both internal spaces but one containing the other. Like Russian dolls. The innermost space, with its legacy of secrecy, of darkness—both actual and symbolic. More enigmatic than the third-space. The tactics for escape from external narratives are expanding. Objects with bodies have an advantage.

Here I have to make a confession: the object I am presenting below, is designed and built as a part of the first generation in Berkeley. Very early in my dealings with designed objects, I find that they almost always come *avant la lettre*. This proves my contention that if you look closely, objects "speak" about themselves. It is just a question of putting what they say into words. And in this case, the tripartite armoire finds its similes in Ticino. So here they meet, surrounded by drawings and Samuel Beckett's *Watt*. Objects come with shadows. Looking closely, they have both a past and a future. They are never alone, even if they are very strange. Thus revealed, the objects presented in this book are synchronic in more than one way.

O'Meldon's Cube and Root

The majestic armoires that hold—while hiding—a family's "things" keep reappearing, insisting on my attention. Despite being emblems of a past era of transportation—railroads and steamboats. Having been dispersed in built-in closets and when transported packed in boxes and rolling bags, even more things are kept in place. What drives my compulsion to bring storage back 'into the room' is unclear. Is it to free architecture from such mundane work? Reading parts of Beckett's *Watt* is now a daily habit. Sentences, paragraphs, and more rarely entire chapters are now another form of luggage. His wild assortment of characters clearly animates my thoughts on "space within space." It is as if this projected storage, is like earlier architectural work, a personal memory palace of the text itself.

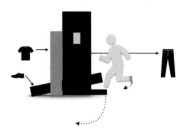

Diagram 6. Objects That Join

My drive to minimize luggage (and by necessity its content) raises the question of "existence minimum." I decide that (for me) pants, shirts, and shoes are fundamental. Five of *Watt*'s oddballs break out of Beckett's text to bring the Cube and Root into the world. Separate, yet tied together, three parts form a free-standing space.

Mr. Nackybal akimbo, football stance, leg back and leg forth, with thrust, kicks a paddle-like wing attached to the bottom of the door. A dull thud and his pants fly out. (Attached to a spring mechanism they are released by the opened door.) As a reaction, his legs are flailing—now standing-in for Watt, whose "way of advancing due east, for example, was to turn his bust as far as possible towards the north and at the same time to fling his right leg as far as possible towards the south, and then to turn his bust as far as possible towards the south

Figure 20. O'Meldon's Cube and Root (Kick-Open, Stiff Shirt, Shoe Tree)

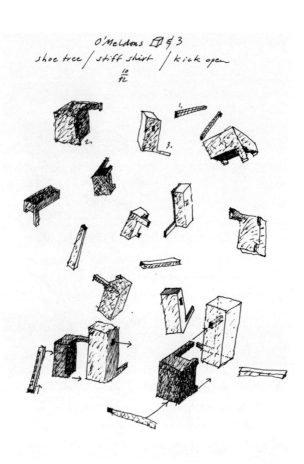

Figure 21. O'Meldon's Cube and Root Disassembled

and at the same time to fling out his left leg as far as possible towards the north, and then again to turn his bust as far as possible towards the north and to fling out his right leg as far as possible towards the south…"[43] Mr. Louit looks through the window in the front door to see if the shirts are flailing too. Mr. MacStern opens the Stiff Shirt. Mr. Fitzwein inserts a shirt. Mr. Magershon gawks (from a position outside the picture), while Mr. Knott and O'Meldon are nowhere to be seen, but we can hear a phonograph: "Wonderful most wonderful, exclaimed Mr. O'Meldon. What is so wonderful most wonderful? said Mr. MacStern. The two figures are related, said Mr. O'Meldon, as the cute to its roob. The cute to its what? said Mr. Fitzwein. He means the cube to its root, said Mr. MacStern."[44] Once dressed, the wearer's shirt, in a tuck, meets the pants, and the pants touch the shoes, in parallel to Watt's cohort meeting but immediately parting by poetic miscommunication.

The fusion of two closets, shirts and pants, one penetrating the other, and the Shoe-Tree that, fallen, rests in angle on a short leg of the shirt closet is an existence-minimum-apparatus. Free from location demands and, maybe more than any of the other household vehicles, depicting the eternal struggle between the insistence of the intelligible (is it a closet?) over the sensible (it looks and feels like I don't know what). Compact and synthetic, the tripartite stands in objection to the spatial exuberance of the plan. And those lonely people I meet on my walks, whose living room is a park, an underpass, a stoop, look back at me. We all join Beckett's oddballs in "an episode in the Kulturkampf."[45]

Here in the encounter, the question shifts the domestic algorithm from room to contested space, suggesting that

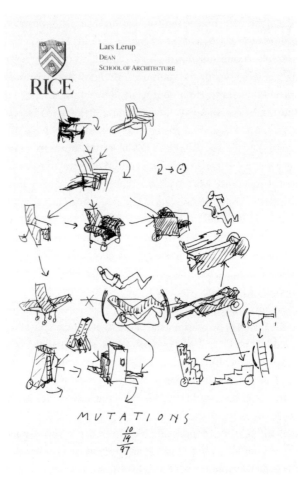

Figure 22. Mutations

embodied furniture, unaccounted for, is political space. An unexplored interiority that unsettles the accustomed categories of the binary outside and inside. While the philosophers grumble, Bachelard returns with the "lairs" that we carry with us, while a young boy involved in another dimension of the *Kulturkampf* sits in his father's closet waiting for his return—in the end probably unknowingly feeling just like another Estragon, absentmindedly trying his father's boots (having left his own).

Spring 1993

Just before Christmas in 1992, I am called to the phone. It is Albert Pope from the School of Architecture at Rice. He asks if I would be interested in being interviewed for the deanship. It has been a long search. The job has been offered to several candidates, but no one is interested: Houston is not a very popular place with outsiders. At the same time, Los Angeles is restless. The new director thinks Europe is passé. Closing Vico is in the works.

I accept and fly to Houston for the interview. President Rupp offers me the position as Dean. I accept the same day as Bill Clinton is inaugurated as President.

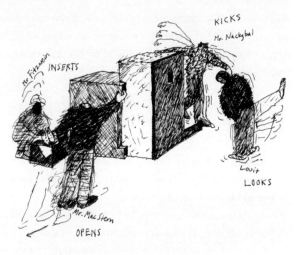

Figure 23. Kulturkampf

IX
1993–2009
Houston

Rice

Landing at Bush airport, you are met with a smell. Some would say an odor. For me, it's an urban evidence bottled by a Big Sky over a wet prairie and filled with vaporized liquids. Petroleum and the compressed humidity of the insect-infected bayou. Texas lowlands. This time, a university car service takes me to campus. Somehow, the ride through forty minutes of suburban ephemera looks natural.

Previous brief studio interludes at the Architecture School at Rice University in Houston have led to Albert Pope's phone call and my subsequent hiring. A couple of hectic days later, I meet the faculty and students. Mesmerized by the panoramic view of Downtown from a distance, wrapped in a big sky, backed up by a grand park, we lease an apartment on the twenty-eighth floor. Before me, the city—if it is there—under a dense mat of trees. This Zohemic Canopy is cut in two by an arch of freeway. Swiped by banks of clouds straddling the sky. Broken by Downtown. Isolated and majestic, office towers pile up at the center (as if told to do so)—an architect's dream, yet the perfect representation of agglomeration economics. Little do I know that three books will stem from this first encounter.

The faculty has many open positions, tenure and visiting, that we rapidly fill for various time periods: Michael Bell, Yung Ho Chang, David Brown, Bruce Mau, Sanford Kwinter, Keith Krumweide, Lindy Roy, Clover Lee, Nana Last, Eva Franch i Gilabert. All since gone, this "itinerant faculty" add in various ways to the building of a school sprung from the city. A permanent faculty of exceptional quality adds stability—John J. Casbarian, Carlos Jimenez, Albert Pope, and an older generation, not quite as enthusiastic, but with steady hands. The school is in excellent shape. A lecture program sustained by generous donations allows us to invite Peter Eisenman, Robert Mangurian and Mary-Ann Ray, Sir Peter Cook, Jacques Herzog, emerging architects like BIG, and urbanists like Charles Waldheim.

A school solidly bound to various forms of modernism, inspired by Robert Venturi and Mies van der Rohe respectively, is about to change; and so is the seemingly unshakable conviction that *architecture comes from architecture*. Steered by minimal protocol, Houston is coming home to roost—a city dominated by developers with architects as bit players. For good and bad, here *the built, tentatively fixed or moving, comes from the city*. And if the school is to produce architecture in its wake, we need to join the melee. For us, the not always comfortable collision between Aldo Rossi's *Architecture of the City* and Reyner Banham's *City of Four Ecologies*. The *compact* European City versus (the European love affair with) the *dispersed* Suburban City. Euphoric at times, the school takes a first step out of the shadow of an elite conception of the discipline. I had never realized how hard it is to change an embedded culture built on survival rather than thriving on change.

Had I read it then, a snide remark by Banham would have offended but also challenged me, since I would in several books argue that the urbanization of Houston is not only related to Los Angeles, but a purer version of a form of urbanism. He writes, myopically (in an urbanist view): "next to Chicago itself, Houston must be the most Miesian city in North America. ... Almost anywhere, it seems, in the rambling, unzoned dystopia that makes Houston an urbanist's nightmare, one may stumble with relief on neat steel-framed structures with 'made-at-IIT' written all over them ..."[46] One museum by Mies van der Rohe and some similes by Philip Johnson and Anderson Todd lead him to the conclusion that Houston is a Modernist IIT city. For me, Banham's "urbanist's nightmare" is Houston. Aside from his snobbish dismissal, the over-looking of a dominant form of American urbanization is not just a missed opportunity but a disservice to the way we live.

I find *Stim & Dross* under the Zohemic canopy. Published in December 1994 in the journal *Assemblage*, with Kwinter as the editor (and Mau as the inventor of a new urban graphics), panoramas replace buildings. *Buildings can no longer be seen without context—without the life that motivates them*. Focused on urbanization, the outlines of an Urbanism beyond Urban Design begin to undermine our obsession with the city.

One year or two after my arrival in Houston, Stephen Fox and I begin driving through the city. Far from Rice in France, Deleuze and Guattari build new plateaus that inspire my panoramas. Paul Virilio takes dispersion to another level, implying that the connection between building and street is irrelevant in the new city of "protocols" and "processes" (so described by Kwinter once he leaves Rice). In a city of "elsewhere," buildings are erased, everything moves. In the school, *speed* rather than erasure motivates a new generation of buildings. A built Urbanism, delirious at times, clearly inspired by Rem Koolhaas and illustrated by digital means. No longer catering to individual patrons but to a city under constant drift. The much-maligned neoliberal city that built Rice University.

The fateful view of the new city from my window on the twenty-eighth floor shifts my immediate attention to urbanization, leaving my previous attention to objects in Vico—until interrupted in 1999 by *room*. My persistent need to travel is now greatly enhanced by a series of encounters. In Japan, I meet up with Fumihiko Maki, who I had met through Dolf Schnebli and Roger Montgomery. In China, guided by my former Berkeley student and new Rice Faculty Yung Ho Chan, I'm emersed, shocked, overwhelmed by the immensity of the drive to modernize. Add to this Taiwan, Singapore, and Hong Kong. All the trips West added dramatically to my understanding of global urbanization. But objects in space do not go unnoticed.

Broken Objects and Paper Screens

With the opportunities that come with a deanship, I am invited to Japan. Objects in Space are now a central preoccupation, in both urban and domestic space. Tokyo is so compressed that visiting the Imperial Villa seems like a return to the prairie. Once I have seen the Shoin buildings at the Katsura Rikyu, my earlier readings of Tanizaki's *In Praise of*

Shadows and haikus by Matsuo Bashō reveal a 'life of objects' that in the West is never acknowledged; in deep shadow, they form with tatami and paper screen a world of rooms freed from the plan—shaped by other forces, still operative, generous; open to the landscape, or part of it. Like nature in search of the next season, always unfinished. In the end, the built is a broken autonomy, perpetually incomplete. The visibly used object (the discarded cigar box) interrupted, mended, refashioned, never whole again, wears time as a memento, as an honor. Caught in the gaze, the assemblage of a half-open screen door, a broken vessel repaired, a pool of water waiting for a moon, a bonsai, and *borrowed scenery* is infiltrated by the sound of the city.[47] The sound of running feet in Kurosawa movies never fails to bring it all back. If the objects below have an aspirational other, it is in this most passing memory. Instinctively, I had projected *the unfinished* long before my visit to Japan; in my visit to the Summer Palace, I had found it.

Taiwan

If you ever wonder why china is thus named, you need to visit the National Palace Museum in Taipei. Of the 700,000 Chinese imperial artifacts, I am mesmerized by the green porcelain, the lacquerware, and the enamelware. I get to wander next to miles of glass vitrines with greenish receptacles. My eye for objects, leaving their use behind, is roused. Here, color, shape, and material expression leave use in the dust.

The size and heft of Chinese furniture in the ephemeral Japanese houses, left behind after the occupation, is startling.

Here, the misfit dramatizes the difference between the two. It is suddenly hard to imagine the unwieldy objects as furniture. It is curious how sheer size alters our conception of furniture.

28th Floor

Shipped from Berkeley, the first-generation objects roll into the apartment—into a plan mass-produced by the real estate machine, were it not for the oversized bow windows. Against this discipline, the Masonite-clad objects appear as agents of another plan—set to the constant rumble by a nearby freeway. My substitute ocean. I settle easily. *Itinerancy* is the motor for the type of immigrant that remains an emigrant. Entering domesticity for the first time, *Objects That Move* sit around, awkwardly, poorly fitting the names of the usual suspects—easy chair, sofa, closet—reminders of the inevitable next move.

On Apparatus and Assemblage

As presented, all the objects sitting around me have agencies beyond utility—they're all machines. In *What Is an Apparatus, and Other Essays* Giorgio Agamben defines an *apparatus* as "that in which, and through which, one realizes a pure activity of governance devoid of any foundation in being. This is the reason why apparatuses must always imply a process of subjectification, that is to say, they must produce their subject."[48] A succinct explanation of how *O'Meldon's Cube and Root* produces its engaged subjects.[49]

Figure 24. Racer Occupied by Luke Bulman

The strange objects attempt by such subterfuge agency to leave the family narrative. To put domestic use side by side with other uses (objects that move and rotate). To open objects to the world. To express agencies of materiality—oil as a non-renewable with its footprint on everything we make; wood as a renewable material and its capacity to hold carbon. Objects as assemblages of several trades. And always, an attempt to free objects from their dependence on consumerism—to erase the distinction between animate and inanimate objects. Out of all these attempts, the object-as-apparatus will produce a momentary new subject.

When "living" is removed from "Living Room," the surrounding wet prairie with its ancient freedoms reappears (tainted by a persistent blindness to the actual). Currently erased by subdivision upon subdivision. Momentarily a room is free, on the run. The persistent shadows of the family narrative are replaced by a penumbra, a partial shade that uncovers other possibilities. Singularity and restriction are replaced by multiplicity—choice, *plus-que-parfait*.

Across the room-as-prairie, potential material potencies roam. Mobility in your hands, a roamer moves the chaise-longue about to discover new traffic situations. Joyriders of the racer laugh as their elders do the transporting. Contemplating, visitors sitting with head in hand, may see that limitations are no longer walls but conditions and states of mind—our avarice and purported superiority is in question?

Objects That Move

Here he stood. Here he sat. Here he knelt. Here he lay. Here he moved, to and fro, from the door to the window, from the window to the door ...
—Samuel Beckett

Constantly immersed in the mobility that drives urbanization, Houston is on the move. Restlessness, frequently employed in rhetoric, is used here to speed things up, but also to deliberately unsettle things. Furniture is always fixed to a plan, to a room, to a location in that room. An object with a demonstrated capability to move is free from such encumbrances—from the name "furniture" and its assigned placement. Furniture used to be called *meuble* with derivations in many European languages—*Möbel* in Swedish and German; already fixed in the twentieth century, the name still harks back to Latin *mobilis* and the fittings brought by the Roman legionnaires on their campaigns and by the nomads before them. In the twenty-first century, furniture is just another consumer good. By recasting it as *designed objects* breaking with convention, material presence—the way an object appears, the way it is made, the way it contributes to the new geological era that humans have instigated—succeeds name and use. Furniture has no conception of the future; with demands on the imagination, a designed object finds it ethically indefensible not to think about the future. Momentarily, objects stand free, open for inspection.

The bridges, stairs, and gangways of that summer of '73, sitting displaced on the granite "pate", present an uncanny conflict between *stasis* and *mobilis*, between contemplation and connection. Both attack conventions. Each object stands alone in its resistance against my going any farther, compelling me to just stay and watch—but the agency signaled by the next bridge a stone's throw away breaks the spell. Suddenly, I understand what it means to be free from a plan. Attached as a coda to an old village abandoned to house a transitory crowd drawn from the city, this scene and its irresistible agency invades the project from the outset.

The kinesis found in small objects is an internal agency, awakened late in our history, probably in connection with mass production and the ensuing "motion studies." Revisiting the drawing that describes the design of the *Third*

Chair reveals a step-by-step linearity—a motion—that is also found in narratives. The *Third Chair* is the synthetic version of that process. However, the finished chair omits the story of its design (if not the result), such as the rotation of the first chair while applying the second chair on top of the first. Much complexity is hidden in drawing and object. Early work on artificial intelligence shows that playing is not easy. Marvin Minsky writes of the computer-controlled robotic arm Builder: "the project left us wondering if even a thousand micro-skills would be enough to enable a child to fill a pail with sand."[50] We can assume that the design of a chair is likewise filled with more or less hidden skills or moves. When designing the *Third Chair*, the rotation of the Rietveld is the key. It triggers the application of the *Adirondack*. Beginning with rotation, a series of seemingly automatic micro-moves essential to the completion of the *Third Chair* takes place, such as the abstraction of the *Adirondack* by mimicking the wooden slats of seat and back by scoring the plywood sheet that replaces them. Or the use of the stabilizing *Adirondack* legs, but through a type of transference making them out of the black wooden bars used for the structure of the Rietveld. Add to this the hidden but instinctively understood practices: the many media constraints that designing with wooden bars and sheets of plywood involve. You can only do so much with a pile of wooden elements. If, in turn, the chair was to be produced again and again, beyond the prototype just described, all the sequential movements would be rationalized and duplicated by a team of designers and carpenters and their machines. Can we then assume that all involved draw from an arsenal of embedded conventions?

The first wheels are seen as a modernization of the customary legs on tallboys. Invented already in Berkeley, they remain rhetorical until rediscovered in Houston. And effectively animated by another addition.

Objects That Move now gain a privileged status among the objects. For a very simple reason: *furniture must move out of the family narrative to display and explore its objecthood.* If Bill Green, an industrial engineer who has come to Graduate School in Architecture to find "theory," has a role here, there is no surprise: with a superlight car in the *Guinness Book of World Records*, and model-building skills worthy of a museum. At this time, he gives me a present: a small colored etching of a war machine. Caesar's siege tower, used in the invasion of Namur, depicted in anno 1770. Moved on wooden rollers, a tapered wooden tower is progressively and painstakingly advanced towards the besieged city. Armed legionnaires appear in a matrix of openings. At the top, they occupy the periphery. This breaching tower, the image still above my desk, is another central prompt for *objects to move*. But the tower, the body that sits on top of the movement technology, holds its own magic. Rising like a giant missing his head, he is Acephalous the headless. Swaying, creaking, and moaning.

Not yet distinguishable from the clamor of war, Caesar's war machine moves cubit by cubit, turn by turn, towards the palisade that prohibits the sacking of the city. A timeless tower, an object type that is persistently duplicated in the history of urbanization from Uruk to Watt's Towers in Los Angeles. Here in the theater of war, the tower is outfitted with time-dependent movement technology: human locomotion, timber, winch, block and tackle, true to 56 BCE and for centuries that followed. Today, the erect tower has been exchanged for other conflict machines to take new positions, and since the industrial revolution, the block-and-tackle assemblage has been under steady modification.

Moving earthbound objects invariably involves elements that rotate. The rolling timber is not far from the wheel: all it takes is a saw, and slices of timber are cut. The axis that makes rotation possible follows. Both are deeply buried in past times. Explicitly separate, the movement technology is attached to the tower. The clear distinctions, despite the combination of the two time periods, allow us to speak of *heterotopic devices*. Each period opens the perspective of two different worlds. But more significantly, it shows that most objects are assemblages of parts often intended for a variety of purposes. That they appear in this particular chain shows versatility.

The historically unstable assemblage of horse, rider, and weapon finds a new and sudden stability with the invention of the stirrup. The philosopher Gilles Deleuze and the psychologist Felix Guattari, the authors of *Mille Plateaux* (1980), show how the stirrup turns an earlier loose assemblage of horse, rider, saddle and weapon into an effective war machine—a machinic assemblage. They refer here to physical objects only. But such a conception excludes the rider who is not machinic. The sudden robustness of rider, saddlery, and lance is the result of a *collective physio-machinic assemblage*. Not the other of their assemblages, a 'collective enunciation' but something in between—even if poking an opponent with a lance is not exactly speech.[51]

Yet all assemblages are potentially unstable. (The demise of the cavalry shows that war machines are always in flux.) No piece is reflected in any of the others. Clearly there is affinity.

Figure 25. Tour mouvante de Cesar: au siege de Namur et ses forces mouvantes. From an unknown publication from 1770. Original: hand-colored etching, origin unknown.

Horses work well with leather and small metal connectors. But their relations are always external. Made up by external agents who see affinities between saddles and stirrups.

Since horses are not yet extinct, saddles and stirrups remain in circulation. The lance is today a polo stick, the same stirrup secures a notoriously unstable chain of unrelated things. The vulnerability of such often complex chains of independent parts shows how readily an addition (or subtraction) changes the space act.

Adding wheels to floor-bound furniture is one way to nudge an untimely narrative. When used on tables in the plan, it's for internal moves. Small, unobtrusive wheels tell us. But allowing us to eat in bed or making a liquor cabinet movable are both still a bit *outré*. Just like the house, *the plan abhors movement*. But for me these wheels point the way.

A *timeless* object type (table, chair, bed, closet), made of a peculiar wood, outfitted with demonstratively large wheels, appears on paper—suggesting mobility, to be sure, but also demonstrating a willingness to stay in place. No longer furniture but vehicle. But even if never moved, a bed with large wheels is never quiet. Adding fingerprints hints at the direct involvement of human locomotion. Adding hand-size cuts at the foot-end of the wheeled bed involves the sleeper and a mobilizer. Space-acts at work.

Flatbed/Rullebör[52]

The ancient Greeks used the *klinē* (a hybrid of chair and chaise) to recline in transitory grace between getting out of bed and back in. Using it for eating, the occupant of the

Diagram 7. Objects That Roll I

recliner probably went from lounging to napping. Assembled in a U, three *klinai*, also used by the Romans, constituted a symposium or convocation. During these ancient times, recliners rested on four legs; once brought back to the modernist designers Charlotte Perriand and le Corbusier the legs begin to wander into other forms. My first version uses two large wheels at the front while resting on the floor in the back. When coming back in focus in Houston, all transitory dimensions shift to outright mobility, not just by attaching wheels to the bed but by seeing the *Flatbed* as a vehicle. The loadbearing body and chassis of the recliner (made of a U-shaped sheet of thin aluminum) is covered with a thin wood veneer (like a 1950s Ford Custom Deluxe station wagon) forming a sleek casing that carries the passenger, separated from the hard surface by a thin leather pad and a tubular pillow. The large plastic wheels placed around the headrest serve as visors. Hand slots at the feet of the chaise shows that the vehicle is also a wheelbarrow.

Across the street lies Hermann Park. We often walk there. Recently redesigned by Olin, it is a close facsimile of the original wet prairie. Already on one of our first walks we notice a man in his thirties, dressed in black; we run into him in three or four specific locations. I begin to talk to him. He answers absentmindedly. I ask him for his name. We begin to offer him sandwiches. Herman lives in the park. I ask him where he sleeps. Vaguely, he points over his shoulder. For some twenty years we all live in parallel. As told by park employees, Herman (whom they cherish and occasionally help) has named himself after the park. For years, before he reduces his possessions to a bag, he keeps an offsite shopping cart as the wheeled storage for his few possessions. The loaded cart often sits alone while Herman is nowhere to be seen; he too has dispersed centers in his huge living room.[53] Herman and his vehicle serve as nagging counterweights to the closets in my apartment. Like Caesar's war machine, Herman's cart has two distinct parts: the wheels and the hollow carrying cage. As I search for a response, the recognition of Herman's internal itinerancy in his vast verdant domain, I turn to Beckett and his books populated by Herman's confrères. The cart is the only prop. *O'Meldon's Cube and Root* is about to be produced. Herman's cart and the Cube and Root—an all too accidental encounter.

Twenty years later, as we are about to leave Houston, we learn that Herman has died, at the age of only fifty. Having lived undisturbed his entire adult life in the park. Every time I see a renegade shopping cart he comes for a visit.

X
March 19–June 6, 1999
room

As faith has it, The Menil Foundation rents us a studio next to the museum. I am introduced to Paul Winkler, the legendary director of the Menil Foundation. He makes several studio visits. On the last visit he offers to show my objects at the museum. He invites the painter Sohela Farokhi to participate. Her "toxic" paintings will be hung on the walls in the exhibition space.

The Installation

The odd constellation of the war machine and the shopping cart stir the imagination around the installation. As embodied objects, both machines appear headless. One brainless corps without its autocrat. The other one, equally headless without a consumer culture—unless highjacked by a vagabond "with a higher purpose." If we cannot, like Herman, supply such objects 'with a mind', we can give them new bodies with a bit of id and muscle. As I recall, this is how it began in midstream with a lot of luggage. Tony Dubovsky, a close friend, painter and colleague, kept remarking on Lerup's (fancy) luggage.

125

Figure 26. Menil Installation

As long experience with graduate students has proven again and again, design is teamwork. And since I have the fortune to teach in prominent institutions, my group of students is exceptional. Bill Green is one of them—he makes the models. Aside from his generosity and *joie de vivre*, his exceptional skill forms the core around the designing and building objects. Occasionally, he leaves one of his finds on the table. In one case, a pair of binoculars. Freed from their purpose, they sit in complete materiality. An articulate figure.

An erect fullness. A *statue* in Serres's sense. An object with body. Sketches of a consolidation of the two closets into one object. Articulated, like the binoculars, it flexes. Bill looking over my shoulder, is restless—he wants to go back to building. He asks me to step out. Waving the air brush, he warns that the vapors are toxic. My office is "another space"—a subject that will be back.

Raymond Brochstein, the director of Brochstein's custom architectural woodwork and furniture, and with his family a generous donor to the university, offers to build the new generation of objects for the show. I get an invaluable crash course in design and construction. The graduate students play again essential roles.[54] Our job captain, the exceptional Russell (Rusty) T. Walker, builds the hardware and runs the assembly.

Standing dispersed in various stages of completion, in the hangar-size workshop, the objects look truly strange. Normally, the floor is occupied by elegant furniture destined for the city's many professional offices. Standing in clusters around the objects, the crew of cabinet makers, machinists, and job captains seem absorbed. Their work is completed in time for the opening. In the school the first haphazard arrangement of the objects seems just right. The equally unplanned rearrangement still seems right. And so it will remain. The atmospherics of the city of Houston is not far away. Sights and sounds of this outside reappears in Farokhi's paintings and an accompanying TV loop by Brian Heiss and Michael Morrow. The clip captures in image and sound the developer city par excellence. As the ominous, problematic, and demanding other. it always haunts this work. Ben Thorne provides the model photographs used in the catalogue, which is designed by Thumb. Just as we are beginning the installation, managerial turmoil leads Winkler to resign. We are left in the capable hands of exhibition director Deborah Velders. The Menil installation crew lend their astounding competence. With technical assistance from A. C. Conrad, Gary "Bear" Parham constructs the *Wobbly* (wall) in Conrad's studio, to which it returns after the show and where it may still wait.

Thinking About Rooms

There are two rooms in parallel, like bookends. One is brightly lit, benign, wide and generous, with open windows and billowing curtains; the other is veiled in shadows, turning to darkness with barely visible uprights and no horizons. In this opposition hides our culture—its laughs, its screams, its sighs, and its whispers. Yet, as Borges suggests, "reality is partial to symmetries and slight anachronisms":[55] both rooms are the same.

This Janus-faced room is, aside from us, inhabited by objects, large and small. When multiplied, an array of rooms makes up an apartment, the innermost lair of the Western habitat. It has its own petrified landscape, its own geologies operating on several scales: apartment houses, walk-ups, high-rises, row houses, single-family houses, lofts. These are subdivided into rigid domains: living rooms, kitchens, bathrooms, and bedrooms. These, in turn, are occupied by equally petrified outcroppings: sofas, beds, tables, etc. Scanning these landscapes there is a sense of gloom, as if the weather has changed and the configurations are suspended in an endless grin—frozen stiff in a conceptual cold-snap. At the same time, these frozen settings are transitory links in millions of modern lives where inhabitants change, families grow and shrink, demographics are altered. Entire countries join the race for the same geologies, followed by the delivery truck. Soon we may all live at IKEA. Here, in this prefigured assemblage of external forces, the average middle-class family frolics like summer, sleeps like winter, only to erupt in spring while their scaffolds have stalled around them. But for the modern renegades of the family, now living in inventive familial arrangements, the same landscape awaits. We now realize the charade: the available geologies serve the banks, not the dwellers! As C. Wright Mills suggested, we all "live in a second-hand world," cast in formal geologies, rehearsed in soap operas, and now replayed in a digital "second life."[56] Middle-class life, not long past its dawn, has entered an ice age. It is frozen in its habitus, in its schemata of thought, taste, sensibilities, and predilections. Even if we're beginning to understand that it's an iceberg, we still don't see the nine-tenths below the waterline—or see that, as enormous as it is, it's adrift, moving, while its demography is steadily being erased.

Stoically, the subject of the built has held a contested place, bouncing recklessly between natural science and the human sciences. But since their appearance, numerous invasions have been threatening architecture's precarious integrity—semiology, sociology, psychology, anthropology, and lately the climate sciences. Always from the perspective of "man." Domestic objects, because of their peculiar closeness to the main subject, have remained in the deep shadows, relegated and explained away as mere utility. Only with the appearance of object-oriented ontology has a breach appeared in this darkness. I have steered clear of the three Os to look closely at the material at hand—to look, as is an architect's predilection, at a specific set of domestic objects in order to "make room" for them. Not just in our consciousness but as independent others, as silent witnesses to our endless endeavors.

That room is literally inserted between the two rooms, the two bookends. At this point it is easy to dream but hard to find—the museum is the closest we can find.

What's in a Name

In the shadow of this chill, the abeyance in the Janus-room is claimed. And the installation gets its name—*room*. The conceptual clarity of *the second-hand ice age* is not yet wholly shaped, but the vague feelings of the dread associated with modern housing have lingered as suggested since my years in Stockholm. The double-faced room may have been born then. A room (prompted by the office as my bedroom), just outside, cheek to cheek with the present. In this space the walls are solid yet transparent, such that the glaring, brash suburban city that mesmerizes me in the Bay Area of the early 1970s has more bearing than the family.

The Houston installation, *room*, is deliberately spelled without a capital *R*—the double/room as *room* takes on a neutral position—*a degree zero of habitation*. A room, not there to serve the future inhabitant but a (living) room *for* objects. Drawn from Roland Barthes's work on writing, *room* is an attempt—and here we paraphrase Barthes—to create a colorless space, freed from all bondage to a pre-ordained state of design.[57] The intent is to shift, without losing the attention, from the space to its content: *room* captures the moment when the movers have just left and the furniture sits randomly about—the transitory state between the room that was and the room that will be. A deliberate attempt to break the bondage between space and inhabitant—to question status and hierarchies?—the devices placed in room can be seen as words, in light of a comment by John Cage: "Due to N.O. Brown's remark that syntax is the arrangement of the army, and Thoreau's that when he heard a sentence he heard feet marching, I became devoted to nonsyntactical 'demilitarized' language. I spent well over a year writing *Empty Words*."[58] The in-between room stands in direct opposition to "the text of the family" with its expected arrangements of civility in cahoots with consumerism.[59] Thus, the birth of its opposite, the *Empty Plan.*

It is in this other demilitarized space that the work on *room* rapidly finds its place in the museum complex. Now, a different set of codes than the family–industrial complex applies. This is liberating, since civility, the fundament of "the text of the family," is left behind, while *room* is being thrown a new set of challenges. Tensions double because even in a museum the militaristic never fully disappears. Asked to displace several rooms showing Max Ernst, *room*, through sleight of hand, is placed "outside" the museum, beside it, but at the same time inside the "wall," hiding at the border between museology and urbanism. In practical terms, Ernst is taken upstairs for momentary storage, allowing us to make one large room, reached by an anteroom, accessed from the central corridor via a black rubber door. Once inside building, corridor, and anteroom, we are in a momentary no man's land. Freed from the rigid confines of our everyday existence. Free to make a direct assault on middleclass conformity. Yet this ambitious suggestion starts modestly right where it begins, in a windowless room of unusual size but without any particular character, aside from its black floor and dark walls.

room emerges from numerous sources in a long affair with city, house, and home. Though the critique of this triad is of immense importance, it is paralleled by an equally important encounter with an imaginary set of rooms—fictional, to be sure, but strangely real. It is as if the complex amalgam of the three sources culminates in a story about a house and its inhabitant. And what I hear is a strange echo of voices spoken simultaneously—not just by the inhabitants but by the house and its contents. The materialist's dream, a house where everything speaks about itself. As a text, it abates the "text of the family," replacing its dull instructions with hilarity, sadness, and, I hope, a condensed, revved-up version of the everyday?

Watt

The impetus to construct a house inhabited by a text goes back to the early 1980s, with the Love/House as a scaffold for Roland Barthes's *A Lover's Discourse* of 1963. The conceit is an attempt to let the built speak. In *room,* the intent is similar, but also radically different. The attempt is no longer to mimic speech in built form, but rather to parallel the actions described in the book *Watt,* in which Samuel Beckett describes a house somewhere in an imaginary Ireland with a set of rooms inhabited by a Mr. Knott, the property owner, the Watt of the book's title, and other servants—or, more precisely, to find in *Watt*'s often absurd, hysterically funny, and often bewildered agent's speech and actions a way to help undo what I have come to see as the straitjacket of our domestic environments. I seem unable to see *Watt* as anything but a sardonic synopsis of the same world that I seek to unsettle.

Watt as a stage, as a space of appearance, reminds me of Hannah Arendt's juxtaposition of the Greek atrium house and the agora.

While the private world centered around the atrium is totally secret, despite its central stream of daylight—completely "dark," protected from public view, not just by walls but by convention—in the agora the citizen emerges exposed, warts and all, in full public view. This is the only way to judge the character of the citizens of the polis. Our current situation is radically different: the web of interactions between citizens in the agora is long gone, and now everyone appears more or less exposed on the electronic web. The progressive undoing of privacy is apparent already in the 1940s, when Beckett writes about Mr. Knott's indulgences as if Watt is in the room:

> *This room was furnished solidly and with taste.*
> *This solid and tasteful furniture was subjected by Mr. Knott*
> *to frequent changes of position, both absolute and relative.*
> *Thus it was not rare to find, on the Sunday, the tallboy on its*
> *feet by the fire, and the dressing-table on its head by the bed,*
> *and the night-stool on its face by the door, and the wash-*
> *hand-stand on its back by the window; and, on the Monday,*
> *the tallboy on its back by the bed, and the dressing-table on*

the face by the door, and the night-stool on its back by the
window, and the wash-hand-stand on its feet by the fire;
and, on the Tuesday, the tallboy on its face by the door, and
the dressing-table on its back by the window, and the night
on its feet by the fire, and the wash-hand-stand on its head
by the bed; and, on the Wednesday, the tallboy on its back by
the window, and the dressing-table on its feet by the fire, and
the night-stool on its head by the bed, and the wash-hand-
stand on its face by the door and, on and, on the Thursday,
the tallboy on its side by the fire, and the dressing-table on its
feet by the bed, and the night-stool on its head by the door,
and the wash-hand-stand on its face by the window; and,
on the Friday, the tallboy on its feet by the bed, and the dress-
ing-table on its head by the door, and the night-stool on its
face by the window, and the wash-hand-stand on its side by
the fire ...[60]

This particular incident told in *Watt* serves as a mission statement. Elegantly, it captures the spirit of my clearly obsessive
desire to come closer to the things we make. To give objects
not just their proper status, but to use their embedded agencies to lead us beyond utility and waste.

Beckett's narrator gives us a detailed account of Knott's
rotations of his bedroom furniture. Repeated turns that
engage body and objects, while propelling both forward—a
hint of both wheel and cartwheel. Knott, using the room's
bearings (door, window, bed, and fireplace), moves each
piece around the bedroom in a jerky but steady pageant.
Only once every six nights is a nightstool a nightstool. The
other five nights, the nightstool loses its purpose (if not its
name), and with the other upturned objects questions the
status of the room itself. Every night of the week, Knott's
bedroom is inhabited by a flock of estranged objects in

various configurations—all still named, but most rendered useless while being progressively fully exposed to Knott. By slowly rotating each object, Knott pointedly explores the dark side—the withdrawn aspect of each object.[61] Two to three sides disappear daily in favor of three new sides. *Suddenly, he is subjected to the will and whims of objects.* With hubris arrested, master turns to slave—the subject becomes the object. Spatially, things change too. The room—motivated by an incessant change of interobjectivity—is suddenly a mere box thrown out of the vice grip of homeliness. What is a "dressing-table" on its back? And, more disturbingly, what is "it" in relation to the "wash-hand-stand" on its head? Is it this simple to erase a name and a purpose? The fragile reality of home, held in place by utility, is broken open, suggesting there are other realities (questioning, in turn, the whole business of reality). With constant interobjective change, the bearings of home are blown. A map of space with endless possibilities appears, and *room* finds its natural habitat. Knott, on the other hand, has changed his position, too—not just by moving about in his room, but by changing his very status: he is now another object of this *danse macabre.*

However comical this sounds, Knott's sequence is an exquisite demonstration, not just of how the most private is in full view, but how we have lost control to become attributes of our settings—literally slaves to our objects, rooms, apartments, and cities. The dusting, the polishing, the adjusting, all to achieve a suspense. As if nothing happens. Back in the text of the family, we are all of Knott's ilk, objects of The Plan. While at the same time, we act as subjects-in-control, who without compulsion treat the world around us as a limitless resource. This confusing problematic prevails. Michel Serres helps us understand why it is confusing by suggesting that when a chair sits untouched "it is stupid; has no meaning, no function."[62] But when Knott "plays" with the chair, he is totally mesmerized by it. The chair is suddenly a quasi-object, stealthily suspended between an object and a subject. This is how objects become parasites, and central to our new posthuman selves.

In the Museum

Somewhere on that map, in virtual parallel with Beckett's imaginary room, are actual rooms sanctioned for the imaginary, usually found in museums, galleries, and the homes of collectors. Rooms for this imaginary are, if not entered clandestinely, always entered outside of daily routines. Seen as a break, as an escape, or as a (guilty) pleasure, such abeyance from routines is often initiated with certain ceremonial beginnings. *room* is no different. Entering from the museum's central corridor, you find yourself in a dark anteroom. A vertical strip of light leads to a crack in the facing rubber wall, soft to the touch. You enter a large, windowless space— an Empty Plan—a new *megaron* in a palace of culture.[63] It is as if you have stepped into a wilderness—a domain usually appearing in dreams—an imagined *poché*-like interior behind the interior you just left; no longer filled with necessary structure but appearing as liberated space achieved by other structural means. The space is wide and undivided, aside from a large, green box-like element (the *Wobbly*, to reappear in the final chapter) so tentative that it is hard to

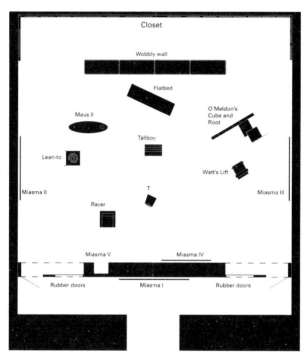

Closet

Wobbly wall

Flatbed

Maus II

O'Meldon's
Cube and
Root

Tallboy

Lean-to

Watt's Lift

Miasma II

T

Miasma III

Racer

Miasma V

Miasma IV

Rubber doors   Miasma I   Rubber doors

Figure 27. room Plan

decide whether it is a wall or an object. Suffice to say, the wilderness is not furnished but occupied by furniture. Behind the green thing, as in stowage, smaller objects and images are fastened to the rear wall and laid on a long shelf. On the perimeter of the outer room, paintings are hung.[64] A TV screen rattles with disconnected images of a city.[65]

Here, the museum guards do not police--"you are too close," "no photographs allowed"--but play a hesitant, ambiguous role. They sometimes instruct visitors in the use of a flock of vaguely familiar, furniture-like objects—"for to explain had always been to exorcize, for Watt"[66]—while at other times they appear to stand guard, arms akimbo. At first glance, although domestic in appearance, the flock of objects seems randomly dispersed. The usual sub-equations of sofa groups, dining sets, and bedroom assemblies are gone. Each object is by itself. Or the opposite, all together, suggesting an assemblage—a war machine attacking the family narrative. When several objects are interlocked, it is an "unfamiliar" arrangement. Some visitors are at first reluctant to "use" the objects; some become more vigorous, feverishly pushing, pulling, sitting, lying, opening, closing, even kicking. The guards watch and sometimes interfere: "Open this way, not that way." Over time, the flock of objects is variously dispersed or brought back together as if to suggest new domestic regimes: you sleep where you eat, or you perform fragments of "living room," while other subroutines are jumbled, broken, and rearranged. It is hard to know what these encounters mean in the long run. Will they pose questions about domestic life? Will they just be a diversion, held in place under the rubric of entertainment? The scene is one of controlled chaos—there is no plan!

When *room* visitors encounter an obscurely familiar object, a physical exploration often begins. Compelled by invitations to handle the objects—grips, unusual protrusions, and unusual openings, provide access points. Once more or less demonstratively sanctioned by the guards, visitors act with gusto and determination as if the object/action itself will take them, speak to them, free them, if only for a moment. And as Serres (and later Bruno Latour) suggests, the visitors become attributes of the objects which, like the football, now as a quasi-object, force players to follow the rules, and force the audience to follow the ball.

As it appears in retrospect, *room* is a foreign assemblage, a surplus, "deterritorialized" and fleeing from the habitual, shaped by a long history of doubt—lived as well as observed—motivated by a long-standing assault on the single-family house, on domesticity, first launched in *Planned Assaults* in 1987, in which the "home" and its equipment ask: Why dining rooms when everyone eats in the kitchen? Why the predictable uniformity? Why the lack of invention, change, and reflection of the times, aside from the same rooms being filled with greater evidence of consumption? The domestic landscape is unmoving, like the author's—I can still here the twang when ice cracks. At this point *room* is one of several installments. Now that we've made the startling realization that the world has become an immense interlocked interior, including not just the old interiors but the domestic exterior they sit in, the now domesticated wilderness has come into view, indeed the domesticated planet itself. The stale air of the past is invaded by a new turbulence—not just time and space, but a sense for movement, a call to cut loose. Maybe a last valiant attempt to find a new place, but as Herman the vagabond lived, this time around we have to tread lightly and our *room* is a large spherical landscape.

**

As mentioned above, the Menil Foundation goes through a major restructuring with Paul Winkler and my friend Miles Glazer leaving; the show, magnificently staged and open to a large audience, has little afterlife. Aaron Betsky, the curator of design at San Francisco Museum of Modern Art, changes this when he acquires several pieces for the museum.

XI
Five of Nine
Two Decades

The nine objects shown in the installation—*Racer, T-chair, Tallboy, O'Meldon's Cube and Root, Lean-To, Flatbed, Watt's Lift, Maus* and *Wobbly*—are conceived at different times and occasionally in direct connection with my personal experience. Thus, the tension between the diachronic

Diagram 8. Objects That Roll II

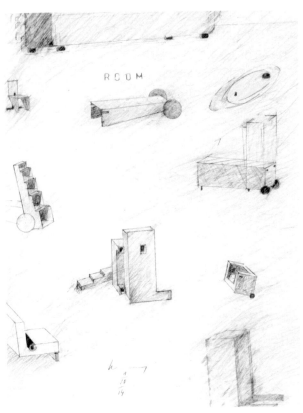

Figure 28. Ten Objects

and synchronic organization in an autobiographical story poses dilemmas. The description below contains only four objects—*Racer*, *Maus*, *Lean-To*, and *Watt's Lift*. The missing five, developed at earlier times in connection with particular situations are placed in those chapters. In turn, suggesting that the objects are *event bound* rather than time dependent.

Racer

There is one chair that I am particularly fond of. Originally found in English clubs, closely bound to bourgeois culture, today it has wandered out from the plan and "furniture" to become a prized object, briefly gentrifying the most bohemian lofts—often worn, tired, and full of its magical presence. Known as "the leather club chair," it is always brown. To my mind, it is a full-fledged object. The *Racer* is a cultural crash. Designed somewhere between the London pub and the Los Angeles lowrider—nose down, close to the ground, ready to bounce, heave, and warp—the *Racer* waits for modern robotics.

Leaning rakishly forward, outfitted with two back wheels, the *Racer* is a square brown wooden box. The seat is a shaped aluminum sheet, leaning comfortably backwards inside the box. Hand-grips are cut on each side of the box at its front. A member of *Objects That Move and Rotate*—unlike its stolid leather referent meant to be forever still—the *Racer* is always ready to go.

Figure 29. Racer

Maus

In a modern living room, one of the central attractors is the flat surface elevated above the floor known as "the coffee table," surrounded by an archipelago of objects such as lamps, sofas, and easy chairs. Elevated surfaces have served human gatherings for a very long time. Appropriately shaped, the surface accommodates the placement of smaller objects, while bringing together and separating the people occupying the surrounding seats. Innocuous and expected, the coffee table slips soundlessly into the conversation. Yet it is time to acknowledge that this ensemble of objects sets in motion the conversation that has lasted since the first gathering around the fire—where the open fire was the first object that brought us together to talk.

The *Maus* takes its shape from many well-known oblong coffee tables developed since the beginning of the last century under the rubric of modern furniture. But like the ancient fire our shape invites uninvited guests: the surfboard, the skateboard, the ironing board. With these devices, legs and wheels demand attention. The already present ball and T step forth. Combined, a new set of worlds arrives: the bowling alley, complete with the ball and one resistant pin; the palette with a hole for a very large thumb; and, because of the protruding segment of a movable ball, a computer mouse. Suddenly, the flat surface is an ambiguous mixture of formally similar yet distinctly different everyday devices. And since the surface sits intentionally low to the floor, the *Maus* is judged impractical. (Designers can only cause so much trouble.) It is now replaced and hung by its hole on an aluminum peg on the wall in the manner

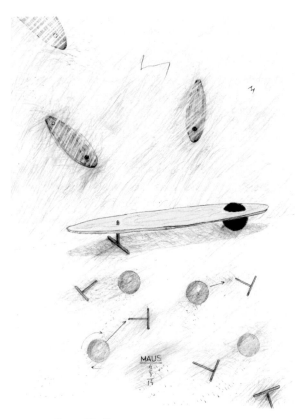

Figure 30. Maus

Diagram 9. Objects That Roll III

of Shaker furniture. Momentarily defeated, but crawling with stories, it now broadcasts from a vertical position.

Objects That Lean

Objects that meet, move, and rotate are obviously vehicular but when an erect piece stands before us, while leaning, we react physically. It is not just a vertical, but a figure that mimics—an undeveloped double. Another figure that swerves harbors the vestige of vertigo—what we feel as 'a swimming in the head.' This peculiar dual pull on imagination and body has led to a long array of designed objects, tilting forward and backward. As told before, they appear early.

First in human form, then as a leaning fireplace and now as a tilt of *Lean-Tos*.

Tallboys[67]

The *Tallboy*, named if not originating on the Green Isle, appeared first in *Watt* and has travelled with us since. Traditionally, the tallboy has four spindly legs, often bowed: a hint of gravity or as if weighed down by the stack of five to seven drawers and sometimes a wardrobe. Similarly, its cousins, the highboy and the lowboy, have for centuries kept and stored clothing in the home.

Diagram 10. Objects That Lean II

Figure 31. Lean-to

Figure 32. Tallboy

Tallboy #1—striped, zebra-like—leans forward thanks to a pair of shining metal wheels (or bowling balls) attached to its rear, while when rotated backward, describing the entire arc from lean to stand to rest, it turns into a coffin. Another domestic war machine invading the staid "text of the family." By leaning into its user's personal space, #1 pokes into the everyday, signaling its presence—solicitous, but surprising by swinging forth like a plumb bob upon opening, a softer "self." Wheeled and raked, the *Tallboy* hides its customary five-stack of drawers inside the visible tower, behind a single door. Made of a continuous sheet of gray felt, the "drawers" form a snake shape with its "shelves" opening alternately towards front and back. Parallel to the wheel axis at the bottom of the tower, balanced on an identical aluminum pole, centered at the top of the wardrobe, the "snake" swings out once the door is opened. Gently exposed clothing is delivered in the front drawers, while more private wear is hidden from sight in the drawers facing the back. Joining "objects with a body," this container discombobulates the traditional tallboy by disguising the stacked shelves in a leaning and rotating box on wheels. Shape-shifting, layered, and wheeled, #1 on its back ends up as a coffin patiently waiting.

A wheeled object, leaning against the wall, sits unmoving in our corridor. It jets out into everybody's path. But so gently that everyone's navigation just swirls an inch or two. For anyone who cares to look closely, the *Tallboy* speaks. A quest for the same, for similarities, for correspondences and familiarities among things. Quixotically, *Tallboy* rolls through the plan in search of resemblances of things, such as the resemblance between a bookcase and a wheelbarrow. Absurd in a plan that is obsessed with difference. Surmising from Michel

Diagram 11. Objects That Lean III

Foucault,[68] mine is an old-fashioned search, particularly when pursued in a grammar of space totally dependent on identity and difference—exemplary of our modern era. My La Mancha is this terrain. Yet, by using the plan's own weaponry, I employ difference too—but of a different kind. Here, the pockmarked veneer was once infected by wood worm— Saint Sebastian's arrow-riddled figure. Handgrips cut through the surface, add penetration to the injured body— the threatened books are behind. The burn-marked plywood surface (harvested after a forest fire) brings Ray Bradbury's *Fahrenheit 451* of 1953 to the scene.[69] In Truffaut's film adaption in 1966, Oscar Werner as Guy Montag climbs a library ladder, "salamander" (flame-thrower) in hand. "Burning Bright." The *Tallboy's* profile is the ladder. A pair of wheels turn the boy into a wheelbarrow. Caesar's war machine

Diagram 12. Objects That Lean IV

hides beyond the horizon. So does Bradbury's Mechanical Hound. In the early eighties the threat to physical books by digitalization is soon dispelled—there are more books than ever.

Formal similarity is a magic design device. Here, the object is the syntax, allowing fragments of stories to be simultaneously 'read' while occupying the same ground. Their unpacking requires attention, interest and curiosity.

Tallboy #3 does not just make use of the wall as a stabilizer, but leans flat against the wall, while sliding down in a squatting position. The most resigned of the two versions, to stand it needs to lean its entire "torso" against a wall, while the raked "legs" and "foot" (bowling ball) add instability. Open to rescue maneuvers, circular openings proliferate across all surfaces. These laminated surfaces vaguely recall

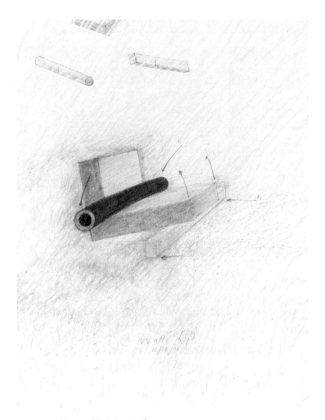

Figure 33. Watt's Lift

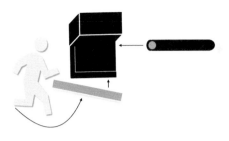

Diagram 13. Objects That Add Up

slices of Swiss cheese. The implied bodily resignation and silliness are defied by the corporality of the object. Despite Martin Pawley's succinct exclamation in his 1971 *Architecture versus Housing* that "an object is not a radio,"[70] we sense the imbedded weakness in the physical presence of these leaning figures.

Surrounded by their many ghost images, the herd of *Tallboys* mimic their lookalikes, while by their leanings threaten to rapidly descend from erect to horizontal.

Watt's Lift

My first memory of the device is a sketch from the mid-eighties. It is a demonstration of its assembly. Hands and arrows show how three pieces make up one easy chair. A note names the apparatus the OIL chair, referring to the alphabetic profile of each element: O, I, and L. The O is a long round pillow made of a rubber tube. The L is the chair proper, made of Naugahyde. The I is a prop made of silicone and is used to slightly tilt the L into a semi-recline. Incidentally, all three elements are made of oil products. At first, I relate this to *Objects That Meet*; with time, I use the chair as a demonstration of Assemblage Theory. Other configurations are just waiting to find their form.

XII
2000–2009
Houston (Cont'd)

Without fanfare, in a chapter called "Household Vehicles," in *After the City*, my third book lays out a house plan holding rows of roughly equidistant rooms and objects. Symmetry, rather than the plan, dominates the organization. Named *New Zero*, it is a double house for two divorced women, each with a small child. The house and its contents are the accumulation of ideas shaped by the *zeitgeist* most thoroughly described in my second book *Planned Assaults* (1987). Formally, the symmetrical plan steps out of the work on my own house at 1234 Stannage in Berkeley. Here, the idea of *the plan as a strip* rather than as a plan materializes. Swiftly, the Strip sheds all marks of behavioral instruction in favor of *equal access* to (perceived) necessity. As in the plan, there is a (strip) of kitchen, bathroom and rooms, large and small, but in no particular order. Drawn directly from "stores arranged in a strip along the street", this plan is an assemblage with interchangeable components, enhanced by a list of Household Vehicles lined up in the "street" —a large central room. New Zero augments the Strip with a linear symmetry: two identical rows of functional compartments arranged on both sides of a large long-room with the entry and a dining table at either end. Aside from the dinner table, the objects literally listed are lamps, a communal mirror, a bidirectional sofa bed, a *Which-Way-Chair*, a pair of leaning fireplaces, and four closets that appear closed-when-open. Seven objects in total. New Zero reveals two types of strips—two fixed and one open. The two fixed strips consist of kitchen, toilet, bath, *Alberca* (pool), room, patio, room; and an open list of seven type objects—illumination, heating, storage, resting, seating, and meeting.

Looking back at the objects designed over several decades, they all fit the initial *list of seven type objects*. The museum is not the natural habitat for a group of usable objects. The museum's tendency is to blunt all socio-political intentions in exchange for an unnatural focus on the object itself. Freed from the burden of proof—to work as change agents—exhibited objects are never put to the test. Once evacuated from the museum, objects are all on their own.

The euphoria connected with a show comes to an end. In the case of *room* the post-mortem is heightened by the utilitarian nature of the objects. Although a couple are acquired by the San Francisco Museum of Modern Art, seven return to domestic life. It is easy to be seduced by the power of their agency when I watch visitors "play the objects" in the museum—here we are all in their spell; but once they leave *room*, the seven objects are suddenly without the directive airs of museology and are thrown into rooms where people are attending to many sorts of things, all of them only incidentally concerned with objects. Those objects that end up in our apartment do so with a curse: will they withstand my test? They must now live up to being "strange." Will the *Lean-To* be noticed? Will the wheels be noted? Will they be avoided, or worse, "not seen"? And will the new objects be ignored since unfamiliar? Bachelard points out: "we bring

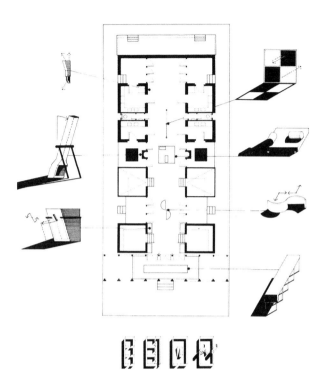

Figure 34. Strip Plan

our lairs with us." With several years of experience, I confess that at best visitors say, often appreciatively, that the apartment is unusual. "Is it Danish?" Far from the productive heterotopia I might have hoped for.

But then there are the few and the very curious who won't let go, who ask all the above questions and more. They urge me to return to the anatomical theater, where a piece of familiar furniture taken out of the plan is unmoored, dissected, scrutinized. The legacy of the old anatomical theater comes to some rescue: with dissection illegal, it operates outside the norms of society; likewise, I must risk taking my objects far beyond anatomy to the outer reaches of my *virtu*—my sphere of knowledge. Just as a union between "a sewing machine and an umbrella" is unthinkable, my explorations below of rhetorical and martial art in reference to chairs and closets may seem equally unthinkable. But this is what happens when you deal with objects that have agency.

Space Acts

Speechless, objects perform their name! Or so it is claimed. But this position is no longer useful: it is demonstrably wrong.[71] When it comes to urinals, coatracks, chairs, and beds, the claim of singularity is at best a half-truth. They do require co-conspirators and our roving eyes and minds. All deliberate objects are forcibly bound to contexts—to worlds—and narratives that put each object (and user) in its place in the larger story of everyday life. In fact, they are both social and physical. Polluted, the hybrid condition reeks of stories. The urinal on the wall in the men's bathroom. The coatrack on the wall at shoulder height next to the entry door. The formal ambiguity of Duchamp's *Fountain (1917)* and *Trebuchet (1917)*. When exposed in polite society, wayward objects are seen as undesirable and weak. The public reaction to *Fountain* is outrage. At the gallery opening, *Trebuchet* is not even noticed: "Must be a mistake; best ignored!" Yet these ambiguities, these glitches of form and name, are now an arsenal. If we ignore them, as Michel Serres shows, we are the butt of the joke. All utilitarian objects are stuck in a prison house of science, neatly separated from everyday life, or so we thought. Objects have already snuck out to perform their quasi-agency. To liberate objects from the depth of this bondage, to release their silent whispers, to fully express an object's *illocutionary force*[72] (promising, warning, suggesting, nudging) is to *find and express* its material agency—the story in this book.

Strip vs Plan

> This room was furnished solidly and with taste. This solid and tasteful furniture was subjected by Mr. Knott to frequent changes of position, both absolute and relative ...[73]

When Beckett's narrator gives us the now familiar detailed account of Knott's rotations, the *list of seven* flashes by—is this an inadvertent demonstration of what happens when a dweller evades the plan in favor of a strip? Is Knott being mesmerized by the array rather than the placement? Obsession over propriety? Repeated turns that engage body and objects, while propelling both forward—a hint of both wheel and cartwheel. We can read that Knott moves each piece around the bedroom in a jerky but continuous pageant—incidentally using the plan's bearings (door, window, bed, and fireplace), but the bearings seem secondary to the perambulation. Only once a week is the cycle completed and a chair a chair—not just a name on the side. It is always a movement in place—as in the rhetorical movement when soldiers emphasize the end of a ceremonial parade by marching in place, or the way Andrea Palladio emphasizes the end of the portico of the Palazzo Chiricati in Vicenza by doubling up the columns at the end of the colonnade. The wheel hides most demonstratively in the movement "both absolute and relative" but also more abstractly in repetition, while much more profoundly in the rotation itself. Knott, on the other hand, has changed his position, too—not just by moving about in his room, but by changing his very status: he is no longer just a subject, but also the object of this *danse macabre*. A non-obsessive dweller would see the Strip organization combined with the list of rooms as an opportunity to shape her own daily life and make her own arrangement of objects.

Similarly the rotation of each object in the list leads the dweller to the object itself and all its unexplored capabilities. Acting on such unexplored capabilities, Karl Marx "stood Hegel on his head," using a conceptual Knott's Rotation to turn the latter's idealistic worldview into a materialistic one (and by extension Marx then becomes the object of materialism!). The turning of an idea as of a wheel? And like the flipping of a coin, Marx demonstrates how a political system can, through a radical rotation, be turned into another system with astonishing upshots.[74] Either way, actual and conceptual rotations are of exceptional consequence.

In furnished rooms, the fittings, whether sitting, standing, or lying down, have a far more transient relation to place than does the room itself. Yet the life span of *meubles* (movables) may be curiously benefitted by their fleeting relation to place. "The Westward-Moving House" (J. B. Jackson) may, at least in part, move several times, while the tallboy (brought from England) that sat in the house at its august beginning, may still be moving now, to and in other rooms.

The attempt to break the forced relations between names and things is repeated in the attempt to break the bondage between furniture and house—the bed and the bedroom, the table and the dining room, the sofa group and the living room, and so on. Despite its speculative status as a thought experiment, it has a real impetus. Visiting the sociologist Nils Christie and his wife in their house in Oslo, he showed the bed on the balcony facing the *fjellet* (mountain) where they slept summer and winter. Just as the bed went outside the bedroom, Christie, in his work, thought outside the conventions of victimhood and pain.

Mobilization

In New Zero, none of the *list of seven* objects has kinetic appendages—wheels, bowling balls, feet (reversed Ts), and runners (found on sleds and as we saw above on *Murphy's Bed*): mobility appears in later generations. Yet mobility is dormant and implied by the non-hierarchical list. Its lack of organization suggests that it is up to you to move the objects around to your liking. Aside from these kinetic object types, hints at mobility in the later generations reflect at least two additional intentions. The first is to awaken the user to their status when they engage with one of these vehicles: once an agent of propulsion, you are also an object of propulsion. The other reflects the urgency to move furnishings away from their position as a consumer good to be bought, used, and discarded. This role—a form of domestic vassalage—is not worthy of the enormous human effort, ingenuity, sheer labor, material result, and, maybe most importantly, the astonishing reconfiguration of the often-limited base materials and their displacement from their original locations in the earth or on its surface. Designed objects are our indispensable companions: not our extensions but our independent others, carrying stories of our humanity—histories that, while latent in the form, are often blocked by name and prescribed use.

**

Objects ready to roll bring us back to Michel Serres's provocation that we have abandoned landscape, place, and knots of human intensity in favor of transportation. What about these insidious and constant reminders of transportation? "*Qua*? Through where are we passing?" asks Serres. In our obsessive forging ahead, what do we leave behind? Now, we pass even through the home, the last knot of what was once our *locus*, our place. The many implications: furniture, true to its history, is again *meubles*. If the Murphy bed in its new instability backfires and you are trapped inside, it is the end of the road—a coffin! Are all three just examples of the "ceaseless answering" of Serres's fourth question?

Yes, clearly, but is this ceaseless query not necessary for any form of reclamation of place? And place, our ancestors' daily bondage with tilled earth, secure house/barn/yard, and moody weather cycles—have we worn out its service, or, better, is place under the current exploitation of resources just unattainable? And all we have left are lives in transport, since what we have missed is that the *constant leaving behind* is an untenable aspect of transportation. If "living in a landscape," Serres's first concern, is the clue to recovering place, we must again become custodians, but now under the guidance of Gaia.

Objects That Transfigure

In seeking the *illocutionary force* of objects, the *Third Chair* keeps nudging me as its sits innocently in my studio. For those of us who see objects as necessary counterweights in our daily lives, this nudging is persistent and insistent. At the same time, the everyday in and out of an unusually self-nudging group of graduate students joins me in the shop.[75] In this "studio culture", generations of strange objects are materializing. The use of the Zwicky Box is no longer conscious but always there. All objects are assemblages, ready to be taken apart, interchanged and rearranged. Once a leg is separated from a chair, it's a free agent. Free, in the sense that beyond linearity there is no trace of the chair in the leg. Yet, legs are hiding in all vertical elements. This is how a table surface turned vertical "turns leg." Separate objects migrate, invade, and explore. Material, colors, and use are no longer inseparable and dependent but free, floating around an idea, an object, a situation. Such transfiguration takes place on paper. The shop is where things are made.

The conceptual movements that underlie language and spatial technologies—in all their varied transformations—are as fundamental as the mouth that speaks, the hand that moves to draw, or the hands, tools, and machines that build a chair. The layered and intertwined practices that constitute the influences—the history, the speaking-about, the sketching, the imagined use, and the design—that lead to devices is obscurely embedded in all of them. As suggested, all practices are partial, like a planet with many moons in orbit. And yet others course through these orbits. A designed "thing" is a constellation of objects, actual and virtual. All are umbilically intertwined in an endless flow with no beginning and no end. When a new chair is completed and placed on view, the turbulence is briefly arrested. But even stable figures are wide open and may initiate, however briefly, new eddies, divergences, and outbreaks. Objects procreate.

Although the initial drive to play with the Rietveld and *Adirondack* chairs may have been raw curiosity, it is soon a veiled assault on the authority manifested in the status of both chairs. Is it possible to unsettle this authority, revealing the assuredness of its construction through rhetorical dismemberment? This question is confirmed by the ease with which each the chair can be turned on its head, and—particularly if left alone without explanation—remain utterly logical, wholly within the confines of the ordinary.

As I've said, out of the shop, sitting in my office in Wurster Hall, the *Third Chair* plays tricks on me. Once in the theatre of design, objects are always in play. Specific design machines involve chairs and all named assemblages. The basic vocabulary of a chair-machine exposes its salient parts: arms, legs, back, and seat—complete or with acceptable omissions. A stable set of pieces but an unstable syntax, distinct but also corruptible. Like its many cousins—the *chaise longue*, the La-Z-Boy, the stool—the chair is never at rest. Because of its record, the *Third Chair* signals this unrest. It is the procreator, the hybrid, the bastard, the (literal) turncoat, the absconder from heritage and status. Unlike its frozen progenitors, the *Third Chair* is just loosely so.

Passing across the multiple stages of our daily lives, objects stare back at us designers. A chair, standing in the corner of a room: unless sat on, it is never still. It disassembles itself ever so slightly, pushes at its virtual cuts, flaunts its degrees of freedom. All that needs to be done is to release the energies embedded in the ancient flow: the campfire stool becomes a saddle for camels stepping out on the Silk Road, only to end up, transfigured, in a Roman *domus*. Movable, objects are always on the road. Escapes from accepted syntactical arrangements are met with media constraints. Stability is one of the more important ones. The reconfigurations are invariably about defection, leaving behind, escaping the codes.

The Fourth Chair

Slightly overcast, seventy-two degrees, with a weak wind from the north—we earthlings stand fairly stable, despite the universe of forces. Although there are four fundamental forces, gravity, a co-conspirator in this human stability, is the only one obvious to us—despite being the weakest, since it

Diagram 14. Objects That Act Up I

leaves atoms intact (while nevertheless pushing and pulling astronomical masses and energies). And maybe it's not a force at all, but a repercussion of the curvature of space-time. Or, put differently (if not any more understandably), the consequence of an uneven distribution of mass in the universe. Despite the machinations of this force field, our bodily agency is truly remarkable, yet vulnerable—strangely *halbstark* (half-strong). Strain a foot and suddenly, a third leg is necessary to regain stability and movement. The immediate other of the cricked leg is the crutch. And it has many siblings among furnishings—most notably chairs, sofas, stools, and beds. In fact, if a foot is injured in a remote house at the top of a steep island (as happened to me twice), a simple chair serves well as a four-legged crutch.

Invented to remedy a range of weaknesses in our extremities, the modern crutch is a bifurcated stick with an axillary support at its top, a handgrip midway, and, at the lower end, grafted to the double stick, a single strut with a rubber tip. Earlier, simpler versions, in the form of a T, can be seen in Dutch paintings circa 1500; the Spanish painter Salvador Dali turned the crutch into a sexual prop (*The Enigma of William Tell*, 1933), prefiguring today's medicinal remedies. The third leg is a constant companion, a blunt reminder of our physical instabilities and, less directly, of our psychological ones. In Dali's fertile mind, the T may have been the representation of critique in his paranoid-critical universe, while the paranoid took surreal form. With my progressive concern for our environmental aggression, I have found myself increasingly paranoid and critical. The *Fourth Chair's* illocution reflects this.

The three chairs, the *Red Blue* and the *Adirondack* with their fixed syntaxes and the *Third Chair* as the agitator of their stability, now stand assembled in an open field with the fences gone. The rebellion invites additional rearrangements. New almost-chairs appear uninvited, predictably uninteresting. Yet the design machine is set in motion. Idling, it is a provocation. Viewed against the backdrop of thousands of chairs, the challenge is obvious: can we make a better chair? The word *transfiguration* haunts because of its built-in aspirations to improve on the existing. Recalling the fundamental importance of the first move—the rotation—in the design of the *Third Chair*, a radical move is needed.

As in all chairs, the shadow of the human body is always there. Sitting, this shadow is elevated, hovering at knee height, invariably supported by "legs," even if they are just a rock. How was the first rock transfigured to arrive at an exquisite Eames chair? There is no obvious answer, but clearly many transfigurations are in play. Sitting as a virus. The third leg as the substitute for a wounded human leg comes to the rescue. If not exactly a transfiguration, a wooden leg is an adequate substitute, while the rhetorical deviation is enticing. How about substituting two legs with one leg-and-a-foot? (The captain's peg leg is useless without his working leg, and incomplete without the parrot!) A new T-leg slips in somewhere between the body and the prop. This first version has small wheels attached to the T—this is the version that is included in the first generation, produced in Berkeley in the late 1980s. A later and last version is modified and built as a model and prototype in Germany.

Both versions, now supplied with a leg-and-foot, are immediately followed by two new legs to form a tripod drawn directly from the *Third Chair*. Other shadows of the body's lower extremities appear in certain positions, illuminating our predilections. The third leg, by sticking out of the seat, pokes the sitter at the spine's sacrum—a rhetorical omission with a hint. Consequently, when you sit on the *Fourth Chair*, also named *T-chair, it pokes you.* Being nudged in the rear traditionally results in mirth—the farmer's Old Blue, with his cold nose, is a specialist at this trick. Maybe you smile, maybe you don't; merriment or irritation aside, the poking is a reminder that things we normally take for granted are actually there. Even if behind us and momentarily invisible, the chair and its equivalents' long history of propping us up flashes by. But since spoken in bodily terms—one body nudging the next—the reminder does not take you back to the first rock sat upon. Nor does it make you realize that the dark, splayed leg with a wide foot actually serves as an extension of the spine. A third leg that, with the two human ones, makes a stable semi-dynamic tripod. No, the poke probably stays with the body, signaled by a smile or a frown. But, more profoundly, the rude nudge reminds us that we are not alone.

But the T-leg is not the only part of the *Fourth Chair* with an intention to stir. The *Third Chair*, devious, sits provocatively displaying its yellow surfaces and black limbs. Out steps the *Fourth Chair*, which, with its questionable morals, is but number three's distorted shadow: the yellow triangular "leggings" on the front of the *Third Chair* (fastened to the wooden structure behind) are in the *Fourth Chair* rotated ninety degrees to serve as two proper legs in a stable tripod. Bridging the penetrating T-leg and the two identical legs, a trapezoidal seat secures the stability of the triangulation. The familiar flat back shared with the Rietveld chair, now in yellow plywood, is penetrated by a handgrip. Reduced and easily movable, the *T-chair* joins the army of movable chairs, which, as a light brigade, invade schools, offices, dining halls, restaurants, sidewalks, and office canteens. Most individual chairs do not stay very long. And at the same time, we can hear the whispers: "do we really need another chair?"[76] However, we do need new plans. 'To live like the way we like to shop' is one such new plan.

XIII
2009–2010
Rome

We would be right to call Rome a trap, a light-trap,
just as an object is. Athens and Jerusalem dispense
light, but Rome absorbs it, imprisons, and barricades it,
as an object does ... Geometry has to make itself stone
before the word makes itself flesh.
—Michel Serres

Pantheon

*In Rome, the plot thickens. The director is displaced and the
scene is crowded; the script is abandoned. My forsaken paranoid avatar stands in the piazza, with hordes of tourists,
an ancient church, and its invisible networks. The writer,
no longer hiding behind words, has stepped onto the pro-
scenium, bewildered, unsure who is writing now because
Georges Bataille, Michel Foucault, and Sigmund Freud are
behind the curtain. Yet I am happy to be back in the city.
The distant Vatican, with its messengers in their flowing
black garments, is a constant reminder of the Church's vast
reach and dispersed powers. Suddenly, an immense building comes alive. My avatar tries to escape, but the building
is too viscous, too engulfing. Too old to be ignored. Too large
for words. Humans, buildings, public squares, monuments,
all have been thrown into an ancient city that watches, per-
plexed, the invasion of the moderns.*[77]

Diagram 15. Objects That Trap

The American Academy

Planning the last sabbatical at Rice, I am informed that I have
won the Brunner Rome Prize in Architecture. "We are going
to Rome." Sixteen years of administration, and now a break.
I am provided with a large studio and a small apartment a
couple of doors down in the same corridor. It is a form of suspended animation. The daily morning hours of my own work
are now full days. No colleagues, only comrades—artists,
poets, musicians, historians, archeologists. Outside my window, Rome. Down the hill and across the river, the Pantheon.
The day I walk down to revisit it I am spellbound.

Sometime in the 1980s as I sat across the way on Piazza
Rotonda, Manfredo Tafuri walked by, next to the portico,
looking straight ahead, deep in thought. Maybe the historian's apparent disinterest suggests that I can have the tem-

ple to myself. Today, ten years later, the Pantheon seems to have been the real reason for my coming to Rome. A strange choice? For a historian, yes—after having been worked over by every branch the ancient temple needs a rest. For critics, there are "contemporary issues" that are far more pressing. For me, a peripatetic designer of ambulatory devices and a commentator on matters of cities, the Pantheon, like the Academy, is a safe zone. A gap year in an administrative life. Here, time will stand still for a year in an ark that has seen it all, and which now, in enigmatic stillness, will hold the objects and the thoughts about them, surrounded by Rome: a city that, more than others, presents the modern drama of urbanization.

Monument

Hiding in the Latin root of the word "monument" are two meanings: to remind and to warn. Maybe this ambiguous duality is best demonstrated by the Pantheon's undeniable physical presence even as it is overwritten by the quasi-sacramental technologies of modern tourism—cellphones, cameras, vests with secret pockets, silly hats, shorts, and sneakers. Tourism and all the accoutrements of its own universal space, moving unchanged from Machu Picchu to Rome, dramatically orchestrates the perplexing juxtaposition of the here and then. An obscure yet insistent past, imbricated in the ancient physique, brick by brick, is fleetingly overlaid by the sheep-like behavior of tourists and the deliberate ushering movements of their guides. Tourism embalms and sugarcoats the Pantheon, and so puts its hulking physique at a safe distance, far beyond autonomy, where it can serve as a prop in global commerce. In this process, tourism also sidelines the (seemingly) all-seeing eyes of power, as vested in the not-so-distant Vatican, since they, too, presumably are embedded in the scene. The Pantheon is this religious power's production—a discursive and practical space that, like other concentrations (offices, factories, jails), favors our cities. But not all is well and under control, because underneath such concentrations hide the "imbricated strata of … opaque and stubborn places."[78] The multitude that power never recognizes—often at its peril—performs in those other places.

For me, such other places radically undermine the behavioral artifice of this newly produced space of church and tourist, which suddenly appear as ridiculously uneasy bedfellows. Facing the modernity of the tourist while the underlying strata buckle and flex under our feet with their revolutions of history, economic mutations, and demographic mixtures, we stand transfixed. Are those buried changes, as Michel de Certeau claims, "hidden in customs, rites, and spatial practices"?[79] Disguised, as it is, in the comportment of the multitude that swirls around us, do we just not see it? Or is it simply forgotten or repressed, sublimated by the trigger-happy amateur photographer? Or does it sit in some waiting room in the amygdala, ready to perform its fight or flight functions?

Figure 35. Agoraphobes in Piazza della Rotonda

Phobos (Fear)

The skulking agoraphobe discovered and lost in Carlo Emilio Gadda's *That Awful Mess on the Via Merulana*[80] is my avatar in the Rome project. My twenty-five years of living and studying urbanization have come to a sudden halt—a metamorphosis made palpable by the hermetic insularity of the Academy. Its scholarly pace. Its quietness. Its gentle birdsong. Its eerie perfection. The academic multiculture—poets, historians, archeologists, artists, writers, musicians, designers, architects, and a magnificent staff—a city on a hill.

In late summer 2009, I stand at the window in my studio. We have settled in. It is my first workday. Located just above the entry the studio faces the city. Suddenly, a figure all dressed in white walks slowly across the forecourt and up the wide stair, startling in dress, posture, and pensive walk. Mysteriously, he sets my clock, my pace, especially when I meet him in person. It is my first encounter with Terry Adkins. His steady presence, the smell of burning tobacco, the sound of his horn at the end of our shared corridor, keep us steady.

**

Every traveler has, aside from luggage, other weights. In my case they are the previously designed objects. Without thinking, they always travel with me. I might have been inspired by Aldo Rossi. Driving on the freeway next to Emeryville in the Bay Area, we pass a freestanding industrial chimney when Rossi exclaims: "I designed that." Pantheon is no different, but without prompt my objects are there with me.

All of the objects, old and new, are now descending on the circular floorplan with its rectangular forecourt, simultaneously protected and wide open. In the circle, like most visitors, I am drawn to the "eye" in the center of the dome. The oculus, the light beam, and the wandering *solkatt*[81]on the floor, the sun's writing leaving a jittering sun-cat that sweeps along the vast marble floor. Instinctively some of us step outside the circle when it catches us. My objects like to be in the center. And here is where we find them.

In the piazza, the city returns. The struggle between the men of the church, Romans, tourists, and the poor is intense. Disturbed, my reaction is no longer cool and analytical but visceral—I need a conceptual firewall. The disturbances are many. The Pantheon proper, its piazza, and the bus that takes me there are potential zones of skirmish. Rome, the forum of modern urbanization, is an amalgamation of contradictions. As its apprentice, my own sense of urban fatigue compels me to draw some lines—to define a theater of operations. Conveniently simple under the circumstances.

The temple, the portico, and the Piazza de Rotonda: circle, hinge, rectangle. A geometry in stone, not yet flesh, as in the instructions of the plan. An assemblage's initial attempt to create a vacuum. It proves unproductive; the result is a firewall, much like a sieve. Populated in my dream by agoraphobes sticking close to the perimeter. Affected by the atmosphere of Carlo Emilio Gadda's *Mess*, the boxes remain in the circle; a set of newcomers populate the rectangle.

Objects (Trovê)

Inside "my" Pantheon we find some of the usual suspects. There is no need to repeat previous commentary. The new abode brings its own text. A context the objects cannot escape. I hope leaving them in limbo—a distinct Roman sprezzatura (nonchalance)—will allow the objects to spin a narrative that can, like a gas, *expand* over Rome—its forum, its street, its public spaces—and *contract* in the temple (Serres).

The *Which-Way-Chair* gives us time to talk; the Which-Way-Mirror allows us to fuse (my legs and your top, your legs and my top); the Water Bed will allow me to merge with the rising Tiber; and Freud, when he finally suppresses his fear, can saddle a mobile for himself and his patient, a vehicle that serves as one side of a confessional Janus, the other side a series of confessionals. Every church in the Eternal City has these houses within the house. (The Ticino armoires are their closest doubles.)

The portico serves as the transitory link between the interior and the exterior. Here, the free writing is met by open space. Rome is just on the other side of the fire wall. The first object is transitory. It does not quite know where to go. Spawned as the opposite of the box, the Sack holds the folds of that which cannot yet be held in place. Serres writes: "Now if there is a logic of boxes, perhaps there is a logic of sacks."[82] While the sacks hold their secrets, the logic that gives the objects a foothold is the ensemble of the tripartite space. The *Piazza Rotonda* expands the territory for the erect torso of Acephalous with his severed head on the ground—the reminder of the thousands of broken torsos

Figure 36. Acephalous in Piazza della Rotonda

mended by steel clamps that sit and lie about in the city; for the Poplar Row, a miniature line of poplar trees cast in some indeterminate metal that brings the Roman countryside to the piazza; for the Rowster, a relative of the ice-yachts of my youth, that assist agoraphobes in "rowing" sheltered across the piazza; for *La Lupa*, the she-wolf who suckles Romulus and Remus in a flat mosaic, her muzzle replaced by a bucket with nostrils and her mouth painted in blue. Sitting about with no apparent logic, the scattered objects employ a soft logic. Here, the web that makes it an assemblage is instinctual and experimental. The hope is that a spontaneous opera will result—one where the creak of rowing gear will join the rustle of leaves, the tragic broken bodies, and the whispers of scattered conversations.

Diagram 16. Objects That Assemble

Entering under the portico with its military enfilade of columns brought by barge from Egypt, we leave the expansive piazza to re-enter the confines of the circular foothold of the domed temple. An enfilade of a circular, domed receptacle, a portico, and a piazza, littered by remains—texts, objects, images, memories. A very brief personal history of a life in a city like no other. Like so much of my work, fragments are drawn together to form an ensemble in a theater. Always with a *sewing machine and an umbrella* reminding me how unthinkable assemblages are born outside the plan. A type of soft logic where the web that makes it an assemblage is fluid, speculative, and often wishful. I once asked my uncle Gösta why he took seven years to complete his *fil.kand* at Lund University: "I read the footnotes." Another kind of soft logic.

XIV
2011–2017
Houston–Berlin

Dessau and Berlin

After a decade of sporadic visits, an accidental meeting in Houston with Alfred Jacoby, the director of the Dessau Institute of Architecture (DIA), leads to an additional decade of occasional engagement in Germany. Gunnar Hartmann, a Rice graduate and colleague at DIA, asks me to join his PhD committee, chaired by Wolfgang Schäffner, at Humboldt University in Berlin. During this time, he and Horst Bredekamp develop a research program called Image Knowledge and Gestaltung. Submitting the project to a national university competition, they win a Cluster of Excellence Grant in 2016 and invite me as a visiting researcher to a section of the program known as the Experimental Lab run by Henrike Rabe. Along with several PhD candidates from a variety of disciplines, Friedrich Schmidgall joins me to work on *Objects That Meet*. I choose chairs again, but now the type of institutional chairs that wander around the lecture halls of university buildings.

There are less glamorous places than museums for objects to meet. In the backwaters of conspicuous consumption, a visible second-hand market is found, often along special streets or districts in most large cities. But there is also the

Figure 37. Tieranatomisches Theater

more or less hidden transitory world of basements and attics from house to institution. This is where displaced but not yet discarded objects are found. In Berlin we find a stack of twelve chairs in the storage of Humboldt University. Much like a crypt, institutional storage is the waiting area for the dumpster. For the recycler it is a goldmine. Already intimately entangled, the stack shows promise. The chair is probably one of the most transitory objects in any institution—changes in the administration? Change the furniture! Our chairs are made of bent steel tubes and plywood. They step out of the 1950s with the spirit of the Eameses written all over them. Here, I find a home for the "Strange Objects" built at the Lab and demonstrated at Humboldt's Tieranatomisches Theater.

At this time, Gunnar Hartmann; Harun Badakshi, an oncologist at The Charité—Universitätsmedizin Berlin; and I instigate a research project sponsored by DIA and financed

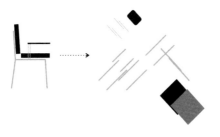

Diagram 17. Objects That Disassemble

by Fresenius Medical Care, under the rubric "Health and Design." In the meantime, Hartmann, trained as sculptor, and I begin an ongoing collaboration around strange objects. With the closure of the Excellence Program, my institutional relations with Berlin end. The refashioned chairs have probably returned to Humboldt's netherworld.

Disassembler

Separated, the stack of chairs is taken apart in the center of the studio. Each chair displays the anatomy of a veritable sitting machine: infrastructure supporting one horizontal surface and one vertical. Elegantly tied into a coherent assemblage, yet explicit about its elements—rubber feet; two legs held together by a horizontal bar that, with two additional cross bars, stabilizes two more identical legs; additional bars serving as the back structure; plywood surfaces making up the seat and backrest. Clearly synthetic yet skeletal, it is discrete and explicit in its makeup. No instructions needed for disassembly. Once taken apart, the same recurring surprise: where did the original chair go? Suddenly, the skeleton is gone and the remaining bones lie unencumbered by their previous functions. The four legs remain legs but the cross bars serve as handles and suddenly the reduced assemblage is a walker. Further disassembly reduces the legs to mere tubular members. The plywood seat and back become just surfaces. The materiality becomes as important as the shape, the shape more important than its name and implied use. The tubes-of-legs are just lengths-of-tube. It is in this boneyard that we begin.

Freud-o-Man

On a recent visit to Sigmund Freud's house at 20 Maresfield Gardens in London, I have seen the famous assemblage of the chaise-longue for the patient and the good doctor's club chair behind (invisible to the patient.) Needing a twentieth-century upgrade, we stretch and cannibalize a couple of chairs and add wheels and handlebars to produce the Freud-o-Man. It sits around in the Experimental Lab for some time. There is no evidence that it is used for anything but naps. Given time, it may be the invitation to office therapy.

The attachment of wheels and handlebars is a farfetched reference to one aspect of Plato's "ship of fools"—not the political argument, but just the idea that motion may have a calming effect on the distressed mind. The other nod is to

Diagram 18. Objects That Spawn I

Freud's "talking cure," here including all interactions of the twelve chairs. It is embedded in that more than one chair suggests some form of interaction, some kind of conversation—whether the type Freud held with a patient or the kind you have with friends.

Which-Way-Chair

The concentration on conversation and the talking-cure in all the play with the chairs is not accidental.[83] All human organizations have forms of internal tension, suggesting that the Experimental Lab may be an opportunity to see if *Objects That Meet* induce the personnel to utilize them. Reversing two chairs and tying them together suggests that intimate conversation is one way to "work it out." A more central concern is to show how discarded objects can be

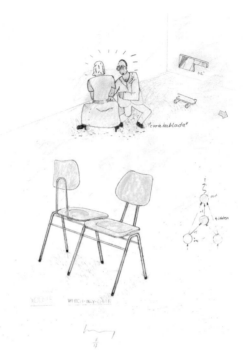

Figure 38. Which-Way-Chair

brought back to life—another Anthropogenic nudge—and to show that disassembly is in itself a design tool. Here, parts taken out of the grammar of *chair* are freed to seek a new assemblage, leading us to eliminate one U of legs by fusing two chairs. Again, this is finding the embedded agency in the materials and forms that surround us in the theater of design.

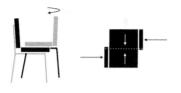

Diagram 19. Objects That Spawn II

Stops on the Way

The earliest and boldest experiment in urbanization at the European littoral is the Lowlands. The successful management of flooding and reclamation of land have resulted in a living utopia, particularly when the planet is facing an ocean rise of biblical dimensions. Although thought of as "a country of city and landscape," it is one *Extended City—avant l'agencement*. A megacity dotted with *urban attractors* deeply embedded in a constructed landscape, threatened by flooding from the ocean and lately by the deforested banks of the Rhine. Here, the convenient separation between city and landscape is senseless. The fusion is complete.

After eight hours, flying in over Holland early in the morning the *landschap* becomes a field of objects. To find a Rietveld chair the size of a church would be no surprise.

After an endless number of these flyovers, urban scale is altered forever—as in the song, "avec des cathédrales pour uniques montagnes"—with cathedrals as the only mountains. Objects, large and small, have entered Märklin miniature railroad scale—freed from shackles like "furniture," "building," "city."

Salomon Frausto, now director of the new Berlage Institute in Delft, invites me to Rotterdam. After several lectures at the Institute (with insinuations that the Dutch flooding experts would have a field day with Houston's yearly floods—but if they do, they will shake their heads and return), in 2004 the Megacities Foundation in Amsterdam invites me to lecture and publish the text in *Megacities Lecture 8*. If we are interested in knowing how a totally urbanized globe could work— there are the Lowlands. If we ever wanted to know how the world could look when everything is made by us—*Total Anthropocene*—there are the Lowlands. In parallel, under the rubric of "Toxic Ecology," I project a scenario in which a mega-hurricane wipes out all traces of the Anthropocene. Houston is a candidate city.

Other invitations take me to Antwerp, Brussels, and another conglomeration of cities in this highly cultivated landscape, the *terrain vague* set to song by Jacques Brel in "Le plat pays," just as my *Berliner Luft*[84] is always accompanied by the sonata of hammer blows at the broken Wall while I am presenting our competition entry in the ruined *Reichstag* building.

XV
2010–2018
Houston–Madrid

The Last Years in Houston

> Has Passaic replaced Rome as The Eternal City?
> If certain cities of the world were placed end to end
> in a straight line according to size, starting with Rome,
> where would Passaic be in that impossible progres-
> sion? Each city would be a three-dimensional mirror
> that would reflect the next city into existence. The limits
> of eternity seem to contain such nefarious ideas.
> —Robert Smithson, *The Monuments of Passaic*

Returning from Rome, I reacquaint myself with Houston. Driving west, the endless matrix of subdivisions separated by ragged in-betweens signals the *holey plane*—the sporadic development resulting from leap-frogging. If Robert Smithson sang, he would be on my radio.

Occasionally the holes are filled, as by accident, by the strange anomaly of mobile parks. They are as if the speed-zone, in its unremitting restlessness, centered on the freeway, is intruding on the somnolence of the sleep zone (the purview of the subdivision)—a rude reminder of mobile America. Each plot is packed with trailers, more a parking lot than a subdivision, and through such tentative occupation the mobile park signals the American readiness to leave for a better destination. Between the mobile homes, the leisurely winding roads of the surrounding neighbors is an uneven Main Street, often just a rutted alley defined by the bows of tightly packed trailers sitting on blocks and wheels, the restlessness and vulnerability of everything apparently stable. The missing subdivision syntax, with its curving streets and clearly separated house lots, leaves the rudimentary organization of the mobile park just another car park, ready for the get-up-and-go. As a parking lot it stows rather than caters to its denizens and the morphology, stories, and short-term mortgages encapsulate the Western Drive. Robert Crosson, a Los Angeles sometime actor, carpenter, writer, poet and friend, simulates for me the peculiar pull California has on the people of the Dust Bowl. In the 1950s, he goes x number of times with his family from Oklahoma to California in the hope of better times. He worked on the story for years, but just like the Western Drive, it is never completed.

The mobile park, or rather its population, is the first to go when times are better farther West. Instantly, the remaining wheeled trailers, apparently held up by the ambition or the restlessness of their occupants, list and tilt or are blown like tumbleweed in the next tornado—as if orchestrated by Sergio Leone. It seems clear that volatile weather eruptions knew long before house builders that building on weak foundations is perilous.

As the opposite of the subdivision, the mobile park is the Empty Plan. Here, neighborliness is not orchestrated with "good fences" but simply ignored. Yet some form of camaraderie is a necessity— proximity, if nothing else, sees to that. Seen from the outside, despite the packing of boxes, an emptiness prevails (a vacuum that across the fence in the subdivision is crammed with programmed narratives). The same vacancy sensed in a photograph of an ad hoc assembly of the strange objects in the room exhibition at the Menil Foundation. It is an expectant emptiness, whispering for agency—here everything is tentative and in waiting.

After almost a decade of teaching a seminar on the Holey Plane, while being surrounded by the objects in my apartment, running in parallel, the two worlds mingle—two unregulated fields with scattered objects. The year is 2010. Yearly visits to Madrid are the antidote. Here, the city is in command. Through my friend Carlos Jimenez I get to renew my friendship with Rafael Moneo, Luis Fernández-Galiano, the editor of Architectura Viva, Francisco Mangado, and Juan Miguel Hernadez Leon, the president of Circolo de Bellas Artes. While having lunch with Hernandez Leon, I show him the catalog from *room*. Weeks later I get a call from Madrid.

Following the invitation to make an installation in the Circolo, I begin to draw a selection of objects. Assembled, side by side, without order, on a dining table, Jesus Vassallo, a Spanish historian teaching at Rice, helps me with the translations. One night he calls me and says laconically: "How about *Parque Móvil* (*Mobile Park*)?" In a flash it all makes sense—suddenly the mobile home and the household vehicle are joined at the wheel. My friend Bill Green at Virginia Tech offers to build the models. The constellation of the Holey Plane, the household vehicles, the move East and the demands of shipping, cost, and timing, lead us to make an exhibit of drawings and models. They are packed in wooden boxes and shipped by airfreight from Texas to

Spain. The Western Drive in reverse: the return to whence the urgency to go began. Standing at Fisterra—*al fin de la terra*—in northern Spain, I sense the wild urge to go West, in all its manifestations. But Bob Crosson's inability to finish the story of his family's seemingly endless struggle is also here, in the stubborn resistance of the intense wind and the pounding sea.

Sala Minerva

> As a child, I knew the horror of the spectral duplication
> or multiplication of reality, but mine would come as
> I stood in front of large mirrors.
> —Jorge Luis Borges, *Covered Mirrors*

A wide, curving double stair descends into the basement of the Circolo de Bellas Artes. Turning left on the lower landing, a narrow entrance, another stair, and you stand in an anteroom facing the sala where two short walls hint at a front and a back part. The curator Laura Manzano and I are searching for a way to install in light of the title.

Mobile Park

The title *Parque Móvil* hovers haplessly next to the mobile park on the prairie. They both appear in the same room— one as a diversion of objects, the other as an American phenomenon. Manzano, immediately in tune, suggests that we affix ten identical boxes to the walls in the Sala. With Alexandrian flair she brings it all to conclusion. When every-

Diagram 20. Objects That Park

one is gone, and the light is low, the boxes would shine like Mexican *luminarias*. For me, my Western Drive has reached its completion—in the country where it began.

Each box has a set of circular peepholes and contains one or two models of the now familiar devices. Framed drawings illustrate the design development. Placed in the gaps between the boxes, they enhance the Sala's substitute for the Holey Plane. Each of these tiny rooms, fastened to the wall, has its back wall fully covered by a mirror that reflects the object(s) inside. But Borges's "duplication or multiplication of reality" does not acknowledge an additional "horror"— the "duplication" of an aspect of reality that we cannot see— the back of each object, which without the mirror is always hidden from our view. Suddenly, this moon-like backside revealing an augmented reality doubles our space. A bisymmetrical room appears, but in this installation we cannot

195

occupy either. Three spaces: museum space (here we stand), panorama space (here the museum stands), and mirrored space (here resides the imaginary).

We *Homo sapiens* have probably always lived in double space: one real that we occupy and one imaginary that we dream, day and night. Fitted with *Parque Móvil*, Sala Minerva offers additional spatial distortions both of scale and location. The most obvious is that the visitor is displaced, she cannot occupy the space of appearance. The many peepholes only allow voyeurism of the sanctioned kind.

The T-chair

The only echo of the distant *room* is a new version of the actual *T-chair* that visitors can test. At the back edge of the trapezoidal seat, the top of the T-leg penetrates and gently pokes the sitter. When the rest of the leg reaches the floor, it sprouts a T. The reality check: you may, after a poke, wonder what the closeted objects do? Panoramas, familiar from natural history museums and ship models, still take me for rides in my past. Seeing a group of visitors inspecting the 'mobile homes' wakes me up from the reverie: the *T-chair* and its cohort of 'pokers' each assembled in its own home make with its *kibitzers* leaning in over the peepholes *a space of appearance with a promise*—a new domestic space where the objects and its attendants construct a common plan.

More Ts

Just like the mobile park, the T has a firm hold on my imagination. Whether the return to the homeland of Dali's crutch has anything to do with it I don't know, but there is no doubt that his prop remains etched in my mind. Severed from its past, the T searches for new attachments—new roles. Yet, even when poking, it props up to support weakness. From darkness to light, the first application is a floor lamp, and the second is a wall lamp. Both bring in their dependency on crutch and wall, weakness, to mind and light, to space.

A Plan for Action

In normal use of space, we are unquestionably in charge—all space is for us humans. Even when we go to the zoo. But what do we do when we have to make space for the world we occupy. When that world explodes as a hurricane or a mega fire, we run or hunker down. It makes space for itself. But for those of us who think the world complains about our space-taking all the time, making space for the world is urgent. But what do we do when we give something "room"? The assumption is that this something needs space because it is neither there nor visible, or, more subtly, that the something is not given enough space (which is the case with the world). By giving it room, we get to see it in full: there it stands in its sudden undeniable presence, despite still hiding its backside. To rapidly erase the mysterious, forever inexplicable presence, we name it and give it a place in our

Figure 39. Poking T-chair

Diagram 21. Objects That Roll IV

hierarchy of things. The world in its astonishing abundance has been very generous—until now.

My project, before I knew it, has been standing in for all the earthly delights. The objects are its avatars. I have always wanted them to "take space." If nothing else to intrude in the daily soap opera—an alternative soprano. I, like many designers, am obsessed by objects. They keep me up at night, they appear in my dreams. I have come to think that a *T-chair* is the old cedar box that I found searching the Swedish littoral in my youth. And just like that box, the T and all its cousins carry the history of the earth from whence they come. And that is a first step to bring it all back.

"Room for Things" is explored in the two installations. In each, things are brought to space, which allows us to reflect on their relationship, always against the foil of the plan that attempts to prescribe use. That plan appears in three distinct *parti pris* or spatial organizations: Single-Loaded Corridor

Figure 40. Tired Lamp

Plan, Double-Loaded Corridor Plan, and Free Plan, separately or mixed together. The invention of an Empty Plan is a ruse to erase all attempts to narrate domestic life. It is a way to prepare an empty space for a group of objects to absorb their audience. An audience that is literally stranded with none of the familiar bearings.

In *room*, the Household Vehicles are not on display and set against the backdrop of museum conventions, *but offered up for engagement*. Once there, the visitor is the attribute of the 'exhibit' by being tempted to engage—to become part of the spectacle. A new 'space of appearance' where your 'speech and action' is directed to objects, now to your fellow citizens.[85] You will abuse the *Wobbly*; kick O'Meldon to retrieve the pants; move the racer; or have a friend move you; tilt in over the lean-to? Will it lead you to hug trees? Probably not,

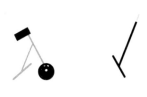

Diagram 22. Objects That Lean (and Shine)

but it will make you a pawn of material culture. In *Parque Móvil* your engagement is different but you are still a pawn. The poking chair as the key, suggests that once you peek into the box where its model sits, from now on you will be poked in the eye.

As a consequence, the Empty Plan, whether in *room* or in the mobile park, changes the conventional roles of the inhabitants: in *room,* the guard becomes both guard and curator, and the visitor becomes both *kibitzer* and agent. In the park, it is no longer a museum proper—you can sit in the chair—but a showroom: you can look, sit, but not drive. The opportunity to give domestic objects such an altered status is confined to the institutional power of the museum. It is a temporary stage for daily happenings with amateur casts.

XVI
2020
Last Things First

One thing is certain: the anthropocentric conception of the world and its many objects is neither the oldest nor the most problematic one. But since the late nineteenth century, and particularly since the great advance after 1945, it has become a most urgent problem—and yet we are also very far from agreeing that it is so. Add to this a sense that the things we design are kept alive by consumerism. Only incidentally are they motivated by pleasure, and rarely by what they reveal about their materiality, making, and ultimately about us as *homo faber*. It should be no surprise then that those of us who think this is catastrophic turn to paranoid-critical tactics. While this tactic has evolved around my work on cities, my side work on domestic objects may at times be swept up in the same emotions. But with my rising engagement, objects begin to *talk back*—an object with wheels has sudden agency. Not only do they move, objects connect, join, and transfigure. Some objects lean. Others have bodies that also meet. Finally, all the lively objects join those that are thrown. For an audience, all this calisthenics is likely an obscure intervention. For me, the objects speak of a distrust of the prevailing consumerist world order. Cut loose from their all-encompassing signatures—chair, bed, table, closet—they assume agency beyond the anthropogenic straight-jackets.[86]

A seductive material agency that hopes to invade both body and mind. Furniture's life as dead weight is overrun by things on a material errand—no longer in our hands.[87]

Wobbly

Fortified by a book on Dada, bought at Moe's in Berkeley in 1970, I set out to close a cycle of objects. To find a refrain, a background mantra, I turn to the first page. It is an incantation:

papa dada nana baba caca vava
  papa dada, nana baba caca vaca …

It strikes me not as total *gaga* (although that word appears later on the page) but as a vaguely familiar multilingual refrain—pop, da-da, mom, grandma, drool, some caca, and alas, gaga. For me it is hard to neglect the echo of the plan. A number of words/rooms are repeated while being given modified topographical/physical form. With this rhythmic spring in my step I enter another episode in the *Kulturkampf* (as Beckett might put it.) I have just parted the rubber-wall in *room*. She walks ahead of me. I notice her because she passes swiftly by the assorted objects—on a mission. Once she crosses the trip-switch on the cord taped to the floor, the neighboring "wall" starts to shake, wobble, jerk, hop, roar, and crackle. Beckett ricochets:

Krak!————————
Krek!————Krek!——
Krik!——Krik!——Krik!—

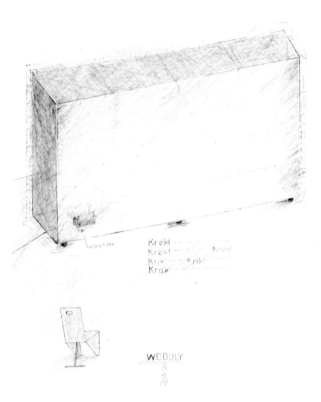

Wobbler

Krek!
Krek! ————— Krek!
Krik! —— Krik!
Krak!

WOBBLY

Figure 41. Wobbly

Diagram 23. Objects That Act Up II

Krak!———————
——Krek!————Krek!
—Krik!——Krik!——Krik! ...[88]

While others are startled, she stops, turns, and walks close to the offense and slaps the *Wobbly*.

The *Wobbly* is the largest object in *room*. Inconclusively, half-heartedly, it separates a large part of the space containing furniture-size objects from a smaller part with images on the walls and models on a shelf. Built by the museum crew as a divider, when put in place it is no longer just that but also a semi-transparent shiny object. A third, or we should say a fourth space: visibly hollow but obscurely inhabited by an electro-mechanical apparatus. It is built like an old-fashioned airplane wing, the pale green fabric stretched over a rectangular box-shaped frame and varnished. As a spatial divider it passes for a wall, and from the museum's point of view *Wobbly* "belongs" to it—after the exhibit closes, they take it back for storage. It may serve as a wall, but it is thick and doesn't touch the ceiling or the floor. It hovers. Domestic walls compartmentalize rooms accessed by doors: anything less is not a wall. That is to say, until the kitchen loses a complete separation from the dining room. The grand armoire in the Swiss villa is the odd ball. In the plan, a wall is always one of four—except in the corridor, where two are missing. Yet when quiet, the *Wobbly* seems not to surprise. But when a visitor walks across the wire it joins the installation. The krik-krak begins. *Wobbly's* signature shifts from *wall* to *object*. As movements go, *Wobbly* is not "an object that moves from one location to another." It is not shape-shifting. The move is from one class of materiality to another—or is it just showing how silly labeling is? The *Wobbly* doesn't change, it *reacts* to human encounters. Nothing new in a century wired with surveillance equipment. But here, the *Wobbly's* reaction is not just paranoid but also critical, while the visitor's reaction is to be irritated, offended, and violent: she strikes the irascible wall, overreacting to an unsuspected menace. Why?

We will never know, but I have my suspicions. Maybe better than any of the objects, *Wobbly* "acts up." The visitor demonstrates her sense of superiority by attacking: *walls and objects are not supposed to act up*. Whether excavated and refined or just abused, the earth is expected to succumb. But when it acts up, the tables turn: vast forest fires, giant hurricanes, flashfloods, heat waves, droughts. Originally, the

Wobbly is the realization of an earlier experiment with buildings-on-the-move—suddenly its antics turn against us.[89] But just as the slow, lumbering houses looked very amicable in the studio at Sci-Arc, the Wobbly's krik-krak sounds like a complaint rather than a call to attack.

Collusion

Since my early days at the university, the value of design beyond utility is questioned. The challenge is captured in my friend the sociologist Russ Ellis's claim that, apart from use, the environment's effect on behavior is no more than five percent. It takes me years to realize that despite his intention, this suggestion does *not* describe the effect that the environment has on us, but *our* actual relationship with it: *it reflects our disinterest in the environment*—as though, after all, it is just there for our use. However vague and laconic, Winston Churchill's purported aphorism "we design the world and the world designs us" leaves us in a delicate balance. Our blind and deaf anthropogenic drive ignores the interactive potential that the aphorism hints at.

If Baruch Spinoza had written the aphorism, it would have housed a much more evolved, and an infinitely more elegant understanding. Gökhan Kodalak writes: "Spinoza unpacks such interactive capacities via two concepts: affection and affects. Affection (*affectio*) is the interactive relationship in which a modality's action is enveloped by and transcribed in another modality. Humans, animals, plants, buildings, planets all interact and modify one another by way of affections. Affect (*affectus*) is the ensuing increase and decrease in one's potential due to enveloped affections. In other words, affects are modifications in our power of existence as the result of our everyday interactions."[90]

For years, before Kodalek brings Spinoza to new light, I think of the aphorism as a *collusion* between architecture and me—not yet an arousal in Spinoza's sense, but *a conspiracy to cooperate*. More aggressive than my affection for the littoral, dogs, swimming pools, collusion might still stem from affection; *affect* (which harbors Ellis' conviction and my doubt before Spinoza) is now the potential increase of affection for the material world stirred by the "strange objects."

Michel Foucault wistfully suggests that one day "man" as our central preoccupation will be erased.[91] The earth does not have time to wait. The acknowledgment that I prefer to see in Churchill's statement would be a first step—instantly negated in the attack on the Wobbly. The attack is a (theatrical) demonstration of how we abuse the world, not what happens between us. Our narcissistic stance is such that most of us will never accept Spinoza's *interactive equality*.

The ancients had no doubt about environmental personas. Agamben writes: "So when we say 'This is a pig, a horse, a cow, a bear, a dog, a fox, a sheep, etc.' the name of a pig indicates a foul impure animal. A horse indicates a strong and patient animal; a cow, a voracious and insatiable one; a bear, a strong, victorious, and untamed animal; a fox, a crafty and cunning animal; a dog, one faithless in its nature; a sheep, one that is placid and useful, hurting no one."[92] The twentieth century erases "personalities" in favor of utility: the pig is "the other white meat"; the horse has been replaced by the artillery vehicle; the cow is a beef/milk-machine that "when packed in huge corrals smell really bad"; never to be seen alive, bears and foxes are cartoon figures and sheep just wool stacks. Yet all those creatures are our fellow dwellers, no longer set against a starry night sky—the ancient astronomer's backyard—but neatly packaged in vast store houses in dim artificial light.

In *room*, Wobbly is just a lonely, once-agitated other, now moved to a storage facility—waiting. All materials have built-in time bombs—steel has one, Dacron and butyrate dope two, and the "vibrator" many. Once Wobbly oscillates between wall and leviathan, it is an offence to our established signatures. An object that distinguishes between the act and the signature, and eventually blurs them. Things we make have finally reached a certain status among a growing public, earned by much abuse, and loved by those who still make things.

**

My claim that the plan gets in the way of modern dwellers is a provocation, of course—people are remarkably willing to adapt (after all, we don't care either way) and at making do. My paranoid/critical stance against the plan is to escape its signatures not because they interfere with us but because they hide what is behind them. As Susan Sontag suggested many years ago: *in order to see, we must strip objects of their names*—of their signatures. The paranoid/critical project attempts to over-describe, to explicate the resident objects of the plan, to undo the reduction that naming implies. Dada employs gaga, the objects perform extra-functional calisthenics—hoping for a collapse of the signature and the revelation of a narrativity—for a story that gives objects agency beyond use.

Walter Benjamin shows how, for the disinterested eye, the art object remains on the periphery, while the art lover is mesmerized by the same object—by the way, *entirely by collusion (affection)*. In the same way, a soccer ball makes more than twenty-two players on the pitch run their lives for the length of a match,[93] to say nothing of the bystanders. Once kicked, the ball accelerates while instantly decelerating, now on its own errand. The cultivation, not the abuse, of the ball and its rules is what makes the soccer game so elegant. The earth, if likened to a soccer ball, will lead us.

Blu

With collusion in hand, I return to the window in the white house on the sloping littoral in the Western archipelago. Turning away from the window, I walk from one room to the next. Through two more, the squared enfilade is completed, everything is revealed.[94] Almost fifty years later it is empty—the content is forgotten. Stripped bare, the house stands silent on the edge of the sea. The abstract four-leaf clover of identical rooms has erased the cultural conspiracy of the Western household. Architecture, now demonstratively separate, has abandoned its role as social director. Suddenly, there is a gap between the built and us.

Once emptied of content, the plan with four identical rooms is a field of possibility. The programmed view of order and intellectual superiority embedded in the plan evolves into communal and personal decisions—a trove of unknown agency.

Figure 42. Blus

Figure 43. Blu (model)

How do we find a place in an Empty Plan? In a white room with square windows in the two exterior walls. In or out of the light? Interrupted, at least for the moment, we find in one room a red piece of furniture. Seemingly oblivious to the locale, it just stands there in no particular place. On close inspection, it has no apparent use. (*Then it is not a piece of furniture*, you mutter dismissively.) I search for a signature—to no avail. Nameless. If it sat on a pedestal, it would be art, but if it sits among us and its shape and size are familiar (just like the bureau under the window in the city apartment)—what is it used for? What is its name?

The dismissal of objects for lack of a use (or signature) is an example of our ceaseless anthropologizing. Adam, who names everything, stands *stumm*. (Agamben) We can't stand

Diagram 24. Objects That Play Subjects

things that are not domesticated. They don't exist. Our incli-
nation to only recognize and value objects if they are useful
is also supported by the sciences—social versus natural science, each phalanx closed to the other, allowing architects
and designers to see buildings and objects as pure form, and
natural scientists to view everything from their "hard" point
of view, and social scientists to view objects solely from the
point of view of utility. But if we attempt to take anthropogenic climate change seriously, we must crack the firewall
and thus the binary opposition of soft and hard—of social
science and natural science. Likewise, if we want to *see*
objects softly—without utilitarian intentions—we must cultivate our relationship with them. We must access the gap,
formerly regarded as a no-man's land, ignored and jumped
over by embedding rules of comportment in the plan and its
assignations of rooms and use. The new gap needs radical
revisions. A collusion between the social and the physical

must replace the former dominance of one over the other. We must hybridize our way of apprehending. Both Michel Serres and Bruno Latour are leading the way by suggesting the recognition of *quasi-objects*.[95] The latter famously writes: "Quasi-objects are much more social, much more fabricated, much more collective than the 'hard' parts of nature, but they are in no way the arbitrary receptacles of a full-fledged society."[96] My understanding of this complex suggestion is that chairs are not just objects but social constructs, conceived and fabricated by a multitude of society's members. Consequently not "just hard parts of nature" but alive on our terms. But this means that these made objects hover between the social and the hard. Which in turn suggests that we must reassess their relative hardness. Now embedded in dynamics of the Anthropocene and essential to our survival as a species.

Such a cultural reorientation is dramatic—difficult if not impossible. Now, in times of commotion and urgency, the silos are cracking and we are beginning to see fusion and leakage, more by force than agreement.

In the white house, *Blu* stands in splendid isolation. And it is wrapped in a social net implied by our attempts to figure out its utility. To find its 'utility', we must enter its materiality, its hardness; we must become its attribute. And here we must resort to affection. Knocking on Blu's red lacquered surface, it seems to be made of wood. Lifting and turning it on the side, looking inside, we confirm: it is untreated wood. All good if it is not lead-based paint. But this is not the whole story: a mysterious object is much like gold—unfathomable, yet magical and valuable, for sure. By resisting the urge to name, we have joined the story of the object—what Sontag

Figure 44. Household Vehicles (1996)

might have meant by the hope for an erotics of art in the place of a hermeneutics. Since far beyond Paradise, we must return to *show how it is what it is*, while understanding that it is Mother Earth we are speaking about.[97]

**

Blu is a late comer to the first cycle of objects. It should have been here earlier as a counterweight to the callisthenic objects.[98] Let's just say it is out of the room, but reappears here in the white house. Like Kaiser in *Blade Runner*, *Blu* is on its own errand. Perfectly stable and unmoving, it waits for us to see. Despite its furniture-like familiarity, it is post-functional; propped up at one end by a short, stubby leg, and "sitting" at the other end, it breaks with most spatial texts—it is useless, without function, just sheer presence and confusingly named. However bureau-like it is, it is not a bureau. As Duchamp asks, should the *Trebuchet* (and *Blu*) be seen as art and thus named and classified? Or, since they look like furniture, are they not just that? Without identity and difference, all *Blu* has is old-fashioned *sympathy* with its useful others. Is it just a chameleon? As Foucault shows us, until the eighteenth century, semblance occupied human imagination for a very long time. Swiftly replaced by identity, difference, and classification, all similia is suppressed by rationalism. It may again be time for the built-as-such, as an alternative to a world dominated by instructions, to open doors on objects beyond utility. Literally hollow, empty, and voided, *Blu* takes up an evasive other space—is the Empty Plan a contagion? Our excessive reliance on plausibility and verification needs a break. Is *Blu* just an offspring of the white wall (an agent of architecture?) and part of the backdrop that we always ignore? Tinker, spy, or a truly modern object? An object that we cannot yet see because we only see what is useful?

Blu falls just outside in the faubourgs of the domestic narrative. Like a broken-off column base, it is familiar but—since useless—relegated to curiosa. In a binary world there is a an "excluded middle"—to hijack Edward Dimendberg's conception—for me, the 'middle' hovers between useful and artful.[99] Blu's identity is ambiguous but the resemblance to furniture is undeniable, since it is only close up that it reveals the deceit. But is semblance the key to a world of new things? In this work, I persistently look for similarity to confuse identity and difference. By seeing through otherness in a patient search for similarity, can we break the hegemony of blind utility? Is there embedded in this rebellion a potential for seeing the world anew—for a new type of camaraderie between "us and them"? Can a modern object take its cue from trees and grasslands that both store carbon and also find uses outside the domestic agenda?

For those of us still paranoid and critical, there is no redemption in sight, yet there is in the life and death of things *a line of thought* that outweighs doom. Here, in and around the small, I have found a cohort whose manifestations espouse no evil, bear no harm. They just want us to see them.

"The Pantheon of Things" (2021)
A Postscript
by Scott Colman

Setting Free the Bears, American John Irving's first novel, was published and set in the late nineteen- sixties. It told the tale of a plot to liberate the inhabitants of the Vienna Zoo.[100] This was not the first attempt to do so. An effort immediately after the Second World War had gone awry. Starved, the freed animals ate their liberators and each other—a parable of the devastating Allied occupation. Until turned upon, these emancipators were blind to the nature of the former captives and their comrades. In constructing zoos, we objectify others and domesticate ourselves. Is it possible to plan a revolution, Irving among others asked at the time, such that emancipation is possible without tragedy?

This, it seems to me, is the fundamental question of planning. Although the issue is usually stated in the opposite terms and as a problem: How do we avoid the tragedy that is the inevitable result of autonomy? Perhaps the answer to this question, however it is stated, requires a better understanding of those we plan on emancipating. The worldview required for such an understanding is evident in these pages—the leaves of many seasons. But Lerup does something even more fundamental in this book. He asks us to recognize the unplanned revolution—really a revolution in our thinking—that has already occurred; he asks us to see the autonomy of things.

In this work, Lerup guides us through an apparently familiar but nevertheless unknown zoo: a menagerie of reified gizmos, suburban conduct, and android itinerants to which we are all-too-humanly blinded by a myopic dogma of instrumentality. Our planet, a bizarre one-room sphere, is furnished with leashed conveniences and littered with feral thingamajigs. We construct and satiate our limited expectations with the former, rarely suspecting they will inevitably become the latter and have had their own behavior all along. To follow Lerup's plot is to plumb the depths of our solipsism and to plunge into a critical tradition with currents that draw us well beyond the shores of theo-, anthropo-, and zoocentrism, toward a beautifully strange resocentrism on the horizon. As we imagine ourselves yoking mechanical beasts into an Internet of Things, Lerup's expansive vision of enfranchisement is shockingly untimely.

The attentive reader may note the resonances between Lerup's work and certain strains of recent philosophy— Post-humanism, Flat Ontology, Actor Network Theory, Object Oriented Ontology. But to categorically cage this bear would objectify a rare architectural animal, its peculiar sensibilities, its particular mind, and its way of engaging the world.

Every pantheon is the autobiography of a culture, the record of its history, the collection of figures it has recognized as important. A personal pantheon, like the literary one before you, is similarly autobiographical: a coterie of fellow travelers. Lerup's pantheon is an odd collection, more a curiosity of cabinets than a cabinet of curiosities. The people and things he's knocked about with and have knocked him about.

One can imagine Lerup peering into our worldly Pantheon of Things. Occluding the oculus, his glazing eye eclipses enlightened vision and a shadow cosmos appears with the fading light. As our earthly sphere darkens, its contours ebb, and we rejoin the universe. Out of the penumbra, forms animate the twilight. Curiosity fathoms the shadows. Lerup, the conversationalist, at first sounds these eccentric phenomena, then projects them—sometimes he literally throws them—into satellites, in order to navigate by their constellations. He is an enthusiastic itinerant, a jack of all trades, continually fixing and displacing himself, agog and amused by, happily adrift in, a sea of passing features.

This is perhaps a strange way to describe an urbanist. But Lerup is the all-too-rare kind. Not one who believes they know what the city is—for whom urbanism is nothing but the exercise of given principles, elements, techniques, and skills—but the one who stops short of that literal discipline and makes it possible. Lerup knows that urbanism, like any art that constructs how we see the world, concerns seeing the world anew. Again and again, he finds himself astonished by habitation and the inhabitants it produces. And he invents ways for us to see what he sees. He makes texts, drawings, objects, and installations as curious as his curiosity and as surprising as his surprise. Cities drift. Buildings erupt. Chimneys tip. Walls wriggle. Tables surf. Cabinets clobber. But even these are only the tamest of startling behaviors, the observations of Lerup the naturalist, having patiently attuned himself to the perpetual aberrance of existence. In his more philosophical and astronomical moments, Lerup expresses the urbs as an animate glob of continuously reorganizing matter—a planetary polis or "continuous city"—fecund and evolving in unpredictable flux. These more speculative visions are the evocations of a cosmologist identifying a universe in the muck. Lerup's planet city is a gumbo of stones and concrete and bodies and gadgets… "Everything must move", he gurgles in this broth of experience, never breathing the same world twice.

Is it possible to have designs on such a soup? Is autonomy possible without chaos?

Lerup is an organicist in the old sense of the term, which we shouldn't reduce to ecology and environment and climate and energy and all other such concerns that our new century forgetfully assumes are new. He's an organicist in a broader, more philosophical, natural-scientific sense. Lerup is fascinated by the organs of our earthly body and the way their autonomous and manifold existence and development constitute the whole and its evolution. He examines our soupy nature with a poetic imagination, straining the solids from the broth and sampling the base. He identifies and dissects the ingredients of our at once proliferating and decaying urban corpus and sets out its liquefying and sprouting parts and portions before us like an anatomist's dinner party, not in preparation for some tasteful future, but in startling combinations with the unsettling power of grotesque revelation.

Somewhere, Lerup notes that you can expect different cuts from an English and a French butcher, a recognition that slaughter—which is a useful synonym for analysis—is an art: a creative way of enunciating bodies within a purview. Shift the blade, alter its angle, and the world is cleaved in a different way, coherent in another manner. But like any good butcher, he also recognizes that the organs of the given body, the varying densities and grains of its conglomerate composition, should guide the incisions; the dissections of the skilled analyst, are as much archaeology as innovation. Whole cultures—of discovery, invention, and sensibility—subsist on such practices, which the artful butcher often upsets and provokes, a vocation of tremendous courage and scarce personal reward, beyond the satisfaction of a compulsion for exploration and expression.

As the trajectory recorded in these pages shows, Lerup is a conscientiously errant butcher. There's an honest rather than ideological sovereignty in this. He subscribes to no guild, but associates with many, and devours the articles of countless more. His cleaver is a well-informed stylus, moved by a peripatetic mind and a piercing vision. Lerup hews our global organism with a frenzied imagination. And when he lays out these articulations, the imminent synthesis—if you can call it that—which he seems to always suggest, means these organs appear like the ingredients of a stew. His pantheon is a cauldron. Quite ritualistically, he makes a meal of things, a magic assemblage of sacred elements – sacred because they seem to speak directly to him and through his shamanism to us. Lerup figures before us totemic metonyms of a global society—the fellow travelers in his autobiographical pantheon—a leviathan of organ-creatures that albeit strange, we nevertheless recognize as the telling species of our peculiar urban present. There's no harmony in Lerup's urban universe—it's not a universal urbanity homogenous and static—just the contingent coincidences that constitute the spatial particulars of a wild coexistence.

All of which is to wonder if Lerup the revolutionary and the urbanist—the exile from Sweden who came of age in the Paris of the nineteen-sixties; an engineer who got his first academic job in the social-science-dominated architecture faculty at Berkeley; who trod the halls of the Institute for Architecture and Urban Studies in New York; and, who, above the zoomorphic canopy of Houston, oversaw the most well-considered response to the most paradigmatic of neoliberal cities—believes in planning at all. I don't think he does. Urbanism and planning are not the same thing. Lerup believes in representing the chaos and accounting for the organized eddies of our urban universe. He describes its strange geology and its exotic flora and fauna. In the cacophony of the neoliberal jungle, Lerup sees both freedom and violence. In this stew of flavors, he can discern the parts and their implications, and understands that this curry is getting spicier. Our urban sweat has become a flood up to our necks. Lerup, clear-eyed, peering through the cute and useful masks, sees the Frankensteins we have created. Emerging like beasts from the darkness autonomous objects of all kinds are growing and copulating and will ultimately strangle and kill us. We are already bathed in the stench of life and death. Other urbanists might picture upright statues illuminated in niches like clockwork, but Lerup's pantheon hurtles around the sun, tilted off axis, swarming chaotically. His Pantheon—Gods become Princes, Artists, Species, and now Things—is a teeming planet.

It is seldom that one can assert without hyperbole: If you read this book, the world will come alive. But these are not the premature, self-congratulatory remarks of a liberator, although an emancipist he is. It is Lerup's concern with the being of objects—their *life and death*—that allows him to glimpse their resistance, comprehend their autonomy, and demolish the domesticating zoo walls that tower around us. Lerup annihilates our condescending dreams of immortality. That's a quintessentially human act of love.

Acknowledgments

After fifty years of intermittent work on the life and death of objects, how can I remember all the people who offered their support? Unless reminded, I will never know. Most of my intellectual companions live in their books—the Becketts and the Borgeses without whom this would be another project. Then there are the makers, whose skills and commitment to me personally have been of inestimable value; most of them were graduate students at UC Berkeley and Rice University. The others were individual supporters, professionals in museums, photographers, draftspeople, and colleagues.

Institutional leaders have collected my work and provided opportunities to show it. The earliest opportunity for exhibiting a few domestic objects (in cooperation with Sohela Farokhi, with an essay by Richard Rodriguez) was provided by Paolo Polledri's *Visionary San Francisco* at the San Francisco Museum of Modern Art. Phyllis Lambert of the Canadian Centre for Architecture acquired a large set of drawings and models in which the first generation of objects were born as mere diagrams. The late Dolf Schnebli and his wife, the gallerist Jamileh Weber, showed my work on furniture in her gallery in Zurich. Kristin Feireiss of the Aedes Architecture Forum included our work on the Berlin Wall in a large traveling exhibition. Paul Winkler, former chief curator at the Menil Foundation, showed *room* there. Alfred Jacoby sponsored and supported me in my many years as a visitor in Dessau and Berlin. Wolfgang Schaeffner invited me to Humboldt University and sponsored my work on the office chair. Felix Sattler invited me to demonstrate the chairs at the Tieranatomisches Theater in Berlin. Juan Miguel Hernández León showed *Parque Móvil* at the Circulo de Bellas Artes in Madrid. Salomon Frusto, invited me to lecture in his various roles at the Berlage Center for Advanced Studies in Architecture and Design at TU Delft. Roemer van Toorn has, in his interviews and invitations, helped me explore many dormant dimensions of my work. Peter Wilson wrote insightfully about my work and engaged me in his own. Ido Avissar invited me to lecture in Paris and published my work on objects in Switzerland. Aaron Betsky acquired several objects for the design collection at San Francisco Museum of Modern Art.

Many architecture schools support a machine shop. The one at Berkeley's Wurster Hall was magnificent. I was introduced to the shop by teaching Environmental Design 3 with the legendary James Prestini, who taught me that objects have lives and therefore minds. A group of graduate students at Berkeley—Michael Bell, William Green, Michael Palmore, Antonio Lao, Jim Zack, Tim Rempel, Tom Powers, and Kai Gutschow—drew and built the first generation of maple and plywood objects.

At Rice, the school shop was replaced by Brochsteins, the best workshops for custom-made interiors in Texas. Raymond Brochstein's generosity and skill pushed his crew to levels of quality and sophistication that I could never have hoped for. But the students were not missing, working closely with me on both content and making. My first assistant, Dung Ngo, introduced me to the furniture design of the 1950s; his foraging in the still undeveloped used furniture market in Houston led us to some great finds, which were directly reflected in my objects. Thumb—Kimberly Shoemake and Luke Bulman—my second assistants, designed the catalog and worked creatively on every dimension of *room*. The job captain Russel T. Walker oversaw the assembly and produced all the hardware. Brian Heiss and Michael Morrow produced the Houston video. Ben Thorne made the Polaroids of the first models of the installation. Deborah Brauer served as the curator, and A. C. Conrad built the Wobbly.

Years later, Juan Miguel Hernández León invited me to show the latest generation of objects at the majestic Círculo de Bellas Artes in Madrid. My Rice colleague Jesus Vassallo translated the texts and gave the show its name. The curator Laura Manzano Méndez's understanding of my project resulted in an outstanding exhibition. Frank White's exceptional skills as photographer and printer captured the mood of models and the minute details of drawings.

Four people deserve my special thanks: Bill Green—friend, collector, and model builder extraordinaire—has built all the models since the first generation. Gunnar Hartmann, intimate friend and colleague, and I have stayed close since our days at Rice. He oversaw the construction of the one full-scale chair in the show. His long friendship, partnership in New Dialogues and weekly conversations allow me a virtual life in Berlin. Scott Colman, my occasional writing partner, wrote the postscript to this volume—it is eerie to see the bark stripped off a project that still remains *Building the Unfinished.* Craig Rodmore, my editor, has untangled my Swe-English.

My wife and partner Eva Sarraga de Lerup has, during a taxing pandemic, helped me navigate my often rocky relation with what I do. Her care, cheer, and endless smile follow me wherever I go.

David Marold, my editor at Birkhauser, has set the tone of my entire experience. His support, intelligence, and keen understanding of my work are exemplary. Bettina R. Algieri, the editor in charge of the content and production team, is equally attuned and saintly in her patience and calm. The copy editor Sue Pickett's eagle eye and willingness to deal with my peculiar way of manipulating my second language is exemplary.

In the end, my struggle with our consumer culture is, of course, a quixotic task, yet I cannot claim to be anything but one fully responsible intermediary of an era. It is hard to leave something behind that, like a side car, has been with me for so long—thus I continue drawing the next generation of my zoology of objects.

Lars Lerup
Houston, Texas

Endnotes

1   Sianne Ngai, *Our Aesthetic Categories: Zany, Cute, Interesting* (Cambridge, Mass.: Harvard University Press, 2015), 123.

2   Ingemar Johansson, the boxer, slept in the same bunk, the year before me.

3   *Bridge* serves as a generic word in the text, describing all constructions used to reach the edge of the sea, including bridges, stairs, catwalks, and railings directly attached to the outcropping.

4   Samuel Beckett's novel *Watt* published in the 1940s will play a major role later in this story, his earlier novel *Murphy* is published in 1938. It came to my attention after the *room* installation discussed below. The name, the rocking chair, and Murphy's self-inflicted attachment to the chair combined with the occasional entrapment of victims of malfunctioning Murphy beds came together to construct a magnificent hybrid, further animated by additional stories.

5   Michel Serres, *Statues: The Second Book of Foundations*, trans. R Burks (London: Bloomsbury, 2015), 33.

6   Johann Wolfgang von Goethe, *Italienische Reise* (1786–88), trans. W. H. Auden and E. Mayer (London: Penguin, 1970), 64.

7   Every time the absence of the other side comes up, I think of Borges' text *"The Disk,"* where he writes: "It is the disk of Odin...it has but one side. There is not another thing on earth that has but one side." Respectfully, I disagree, since every object I regard is missing its back ...

8   Gilles Deleuze and Felix Guattari, *A Thousand Plateaus: Capitalism and Schizophrenia*, trans. Brian Massumi (Minneapolis: University of Minnesota Press, 1991), 414.

9   A dictum often repeated in class.

10   Jean Gottman, *Megalopolis: The Urbanized Northeastern Seaboard of the United States* (New York: The Twentieth Century Fund, 1961), 43.

11   Quoting from the work of Arthur Quinn, a professor of rhetoric, here applied to architecture, we enter the field of deviation from the ordinary: an essential device for the project at hand. Arthur Quinn, *Figures of Speech: 60 Ways to Turn a Phrase* (Salt Lake City: Peregrine Smith, 1982), 6.

12   Already in 1956, Hannah Arendt lamented that "the public realm has almost completely receded, so that greatness has given way to charm everywhere." Hannah Arendt, *The Human Condition* (Chicago: University of Chicago Press, 1958), 52. Arendt might agree that there is an "architecture for the public," but not a "public realm"—a place—as is all too evident in 2019. Further implication

suggests that our work "on small things" is an attempt to deviate from all that now greatly accumulated charm.

13   Quinn, *Figures of Speech*, 6.
14   Ibid., 8.
15   Ibid., 9.
16   Ibid., 7.
17   Ibid., 13.
18   Ibid., 14.
19   Ibid., 19.
20   Ibid., 20.
21   Minsky, *The Society of Mind*, 29.
22   Andrew Bromberg, *Andrew Bromberg at Aedas: West Kowloon Station* (New York: Rizzoli Electa, 2019), 63.
23   Francis Ponge, *L'Objet, c'est la poetique* (The Object is the poetics), quoted in Ton Verstegen, *Tropisms* (Rotterdam: Nai, 2001), 44.
24   A play on Marcel Duchamps' miniature French window called *Fresh Widow*. The *Fresh Window* in the Nofamily House allows children to see into their parents' bedroom.
25   *Meuble*: a piece of furniture in French—here as distinct from the house, which is immovable.
26   The status of a wall for those living in a walled city is very different than for those escapees and invaders who are up against it. Begun in 1981, in the mid-1980s in West Berlin, the Wall appears naturalized, common—an inconvenient backdrop to everyday life in the thriving city. On the East side, the GDR's Antifaschistischer Schutzwall (anti-fascist wall of protection) has a very different status: from here, the walled city probably appears as a Fata Morgana for many, and for others as the necessary Schutz from the evils of Western decadence and capitalism. For us outsiders, the wall is a schizo-object, haunting in its curious familiarity: just a cement-block wall with a sewage pipe stuck on its top. A built stick-figure. Crude, yet formidable. Darkly sinister in its utter simplicity and shocking capacity to divide and conquer.
27   Sheldon S. Wohlin, *Politics and Vision: Continuity and Innovation in Western Political Thought* (Princeton and Oxford: Princeton University Press, 2004), 179–80.
28   Today, it is impossible to ignore the gender bias in both Fortuna and Lady Luck, not to mention the chance taker—*mea culpa*.
29   My editor, Craig Rodmore, notes, also from Ecclesiastes: "I returned, and saw under the sun, that the race is not to the swift, nor the battle to the strong, neither yet bread to the wise, nor yet riches to men of understanding, nor yet favour to men of skill; but time and chance happeneth to them all."
30   The term, coined by Masahiro Mori in 1970, describes an eerie zone of resemblance occupied by robots that look almost human. Generalizing, we suggest that Mori's Japanese expression *bukimi no tani* (which literally translates as "the valley of eeriness") in turn suggests that the Berlin Wall, itself a very crude robot, combined with the expanded field of entrapments, is also an Uncanny Valley.

31   Yet, as the final exhibition showed, we, the non-Berliners, were the only ones fascinated by the Wall. The silence around our project was absolute until, just a year or two later, the Wall fell and the show went on the road in Russia. One of our illustrations became the poster for the traveling exhibition. Much of the disinterest of West Berliners in the Wall originates in the flagrant liberty of the city that kept the bubble inflated. The Wall was just a demarcation, especially since Radio Free Europe reached far beyond the Wall into the other city. The circular enclosure awarded the West Berliner a similar but much greater freedom to the sequestered liberty of the Jews in the Ghetto Nuovo, a small island in the Venice Lagoon; and it approximated the liberties created by the denizens of Kowloon's Walled City. In each case, the ambiguity of the Wall is flagrant. Despite their utter silence, all walls have a strange and ambiguous potential hiding within: did the Berlin Wall divide to conquer or to join, to (eventually) unite?

32   The title of the project, *Here the Time Is Always Sunday*, is a reference to Walter Benjamin's description of the strange atmosphere of the back porch facing the inner courtyard in his family's Berlin apartment, suspended from family life, work, school, and the bustling surrounding city.

33   Jorge Luis Borges, "The South," in *Collected Fictions*, trans. Andrew Hurley (New York: Viking, 1998), 175. Similarly he writes of "the City, at that seven o'clock in the morning" when "the streets [are] like long porches and corridors, and plazas like interior courtyards." Both observations hint at the extremely rare, magical moments of silence and tranquility in the city.

34   Umberto Eco, *The Open Work*, trans. Anna Cancogni (Cambridge, Mass.: Harvard University Press, 1989), 14.

35   A section of the third version of the old Wall, replaced in 1975, reveals a stiff, erect "body" (the wall proper) with a large underground concrete "foot" (pointing in the direction of the West) and a prominent "head" (two-thirds of a cement pipe). An assemblage of "body parts" some 2.4 meters tall—an oversized proxy for an East German guard. Trying to escape (if you could get this far unharmed) by jumping up to get your arms and hands around the "head" would probably not succeed. For all its concrete crudeness, given the physical limitations of the human body, the built other, the eerie guardsman, wins. Strangely endowed with a menacing intelligence, the erect avatar is a true pseudo-object— man and machine. Figuratively, we enter the militarized zone to face the Wall. From now on it is an anatomical theater.

36   Michel Serres, *Rome: The Book of Foundations*, trans. Felicia McCarren (Stanford: Stanford University Press, 1991), 62.

37   The tumbleweed, used in Spaghetti Westerns for dramatic effect, is a peculiar design machine: the last desert rain long gone, the short spiky bush breaks loose from its roots. Suddenly liberated, now on the wings of the wind, it perfects its circularity to become an elastic sphere, both wheel and ball. It rushes across our imag-

inary valley to spread its seedlings by chance and circumstance, procreating while dying. A brilliant example of nature's own physics: growth, decay, and subsequent reproduction propelled by seasonal change and the power of the wind. Here, rotation is the force for change—motivated by the dry, hauling prairie gust. For us, the throw of a ball, the swing, the pitch, and the fling, serve as a respectable parallel, suggesting that thrown objects begin their real productivity when set free from the pitcher's hand.

38   J. G. Ballard, *Crash* (New York: Farrar, Straus and Giroux, 1973), 38.

39   Umberto Eco, *The Open Work*, trans. Anna Cancogni, Introduction by David Robey (Cambridge, Mass.: Harvard University Press, 1989), 21.

40   Umberto Eco, "The Form of Disorder," trans. Britt Eversole, *Pidgin* 9 (Fall 2010), 168.

41   Architectural Association and Southern California Institute of Architecture, respectively.

42   An architectural term defining a confined space, not necessarily accessible; probably distantly related to *une poche* as in a pocket, while the verb *pocher* has a range of meanings from poaching an egg to giving someone a black eye.

43   Samuel Beckett, *Watt* (London: Calder Jupiter Books, 1963), 28.

44   Ibid., 186.

45   Ibid., 187.

46   I owe this remark to Michelangelo Sabatini. Reyner Banham, "In the Neighborhood of Art," *Art in America* 75 (June 1987), 124–29; reprinted in *A Critic Writes: Essays by Reyner Banham*, eds. Mary Banham, Paul Barker, Sutherland Lyall, and Cedric Price (Berkeley, Los Angeles, and London: University of California Press, 1996), 270–75.

47   Barrowed scenery is the Japanese landscape designer's ability to cut out a large swathe of unseemly scenery and foreground a more attractive background. In Tokyo, the barrowed scenery is invariably Mount Fuji.

48   Giorgio Agamben, *What Is an Apparatus, and Other Essays. Crossing Aesthetics*, ed. Werner Hamacher (Stanford, Ca.: Stanford University Press, 2009), 11.

49   In the upcoming Figure 23, note how the audience in the Menil Installation is being "produced by the object."

50   Marvin Minsky, *The Society of Mind* (New York: Simon and Schuster, 1985), 29.

51   See Larval Subject's post *Two Types of Assemblages*, February 20, 2011, under Uncategorized comments. Although an effective elucidation, a third category of assemblage is still missing.

52   The *Flatbed's* double name rullebör is a colloquial Swedish word for a "rolling stretcher", hinting at the many uses of this device.

53   There is hidden suggestion in the idea of the park serving as Herman's living room, in turn suggesting that, regardless of divisions, the plan should have one sole label: *living room*.

54   Russel T. Walker, Ben Thorne, Michael Morrow, Brian Heiss, and Thumb (Kimberley Shoemake and Luke Bulman). For the complete roster, see Lars Lerup and Sohela Farokhi, *Room: Installation Catalog* (Houston: Menil Foundation, 1999), 63.

55   Jorge Luis Borges, "The South," in *Collected Fictions*, trans. Andrew Hurley (New York: Viking, 1998), 175.

56   C. Wright Mills, "The Cultural Apparatus," in *Power, Politics and People: The Collective Essays of C. Wright Mills*, ed. Irving Louis Horowitz (London, Oxford, and New York: Oxford University Press, 1967), 23–24. Mills writes: "The first rule for understanding the human condition is that men live in second-hand worlds. They are aware of much more than they have personally experienced; and their own experience is always indirect. The quality of their lives is determined by meanings they have received from others. Everyone lives in a world of such meanings. No man stands alone directly confronting a world of solid fact. No such world is available. The closest men come to it is when they are infants or when they become insane: then, in a terrifying scene of meaningless events and senseless confusion, they are often seized with the panic of near-total insecurity." It is the domain of this last sentence that room is flirting with!

57   See Roland Barthes, *Writing Degree Zero*, trans. Anette Lavers and Colin Smith (London: Jonathan Cape, 1967), 79.

58   John Cage, "Uncaged Words: John Cage in Dialogue with Chance with Joan Retallack," in *ROLYWHOLLYOVER: A Circus* (New York: Rizzoli, 1993), n.p.

59   The "text of the family" stems from my early interests in semiotics, essentially the "anthropologizing" of the family, a set of complex behavioral rules set more or less explicitly for the family.

60   Samuel Beckett, *Watt* (London: Calder Jupiter Books, 1963), 204.

61   "Withdrawn" refers to the sides hidden from view during Knott's rotations, sidestepping the "withdrawn real" Graham Harman refers to throughout his work.

62   Michel Serres, *The Parasite*, trans. by Lawrence R. Schehr (Minneapolis: University of Minnesota Press, 2007), 225. There is an echo of Walter Benjamin's description of how we relate to art: we are either seeing objects fleetingly in the corner of our eye, or being totally mesmerized.

63   As mentioned before, the atrium—the central space found in the house, and the corresponding megaron found in the Greek palace—was also a metaphor for darkness, for real privacy.

64   Drawings by Lerup, paintings and sketches by Farokhi.

65   The paintings by Farokhi depict the troubled, polluted, and problematic city beyond, the dark side of *room*.

66   Beckett, *Watt*, 103.

67   So named since the encounter with the tallboy in Samuel Beckett's *Watt*—specifically in Knott's room, where, in preparation for night, he rotates all his furniture ninety degrees—furniture is now a movable feast, never again at rest. The *Tallboy* was originally mis-

named *Lean-To*, a name borrowed from vernacular architecture. Correcting this here, we refer to this closet which leans away from the wall simply as *Tallboy*.

68 Michel Foucault, *The Order of Things: An Archeology of the Human Sciences* (New York: Vintage, 1994), 46.

69 Ray Bradbury, *Fahrenheit 451* (New York, NY: Ballantine Books, 1953).

70 Martin Pawley, *Architecture Versus Housing* (New York: Praeger, 1971), 63.

71 The next generation of objects now surrounding us—"frozen embryos, expert systems, digital machines, sensor-equipped robots, hybrid corn," and so on, as listed by Bruno Latour—makes it clear that we are now permanently inscribed in the objects we make. Bruno Latour, *We Have Never Been Modern*, trans. Catherine Porter (Cambridge, Mass.: Harvard University Press, 1993), 49.

72 J. L. Austin defined three speech acts: *locution* (what is said and meant), *illocution* (what is done), *perlocution* (what happens as a result). In *How to Do Things with Words* (Cambridge, Mass.: Harvard University Press, 1962), 101–105.

73 Samuel Beckett, *Watt* (London: Calder Jupiter Books, 1963), 204.

74 Walter Benjamin speaks of a "Copernican revolution in historical perception."

75 At various times during the 1980s, Michael Bell, Bill Green, Michael Palmore, Antonio Lao, Jim Zack, Tim Rempel, Kai Gutchow, all serve in several roles: graduate students, teaching assistants, and shop assistants. Their commitment to and interest in the project have been invaluable. Many remain close friends.

76 This is in obscure deference to my mentor and friend Roger Montgomery, who was the first to raise this doubt, sometime in the mid-sixties, when he said: "Do we really need another apartment plan?"—a statement that probably set in motion my own trouble with frozen figures.

77 Lars Lerup, "Phobia and the City: Rome," in *Run for Cover!* (Cambridge, Harvard Design Magazine, No. 42-S/S 2016), 26.

78 Michel de Certeau, The Practice of Everyday Life, trans. Steven Rendall (Berkeley: University of California Press, 1984), 200. "This is the logic of production: ever since the eighteen century, it has engendered its own discursive and practical space, on the basis of concentration—the office, the factory, the city. It rejects the relevance of places it does not create."

79 Ibid., 201.

80 Carlo Emilio Gadda, *That Awful Mess on the Via Merulana*, Introduction by Italo Calvino, trans. William Weaver (The New York Review of Books, New York City, 1999). As stated, the agoraphobe is found in my unscholarly reading of the book. And never found again. Thus I leave her or him to my flighty memory and to the dark spaces of the book.

81 *Solkatt*, a wonderful Swedish word translates awkwardly to sun-cat, suggesting a restless mobility of both sun and feline.

82   Michel Serres, *Rome: The Book of Foundations*, trans. Felicia McCarren (Stanford: Stanford University Press, 1991), 236.

83   In a project conducted by Joe Powell concerned with conflicts in the building industry, we attempt to figure out how internal disputes lead to cost-overruns. "Most of today's substantial projects, in any field, are the result of the hard work of teams of experts who come together, combine their expertise, and develop new, innovative approaches to problem solving. Today's American economy is demanding even higher levels of innovation and creativity. Team integration has never been a more valuable commodity. Groups of individual professionals who successfully partner with each other and integrate their efforts have a measurable track record of solving problems faster and more effectively while generating fewer delays and unresolved disputes. Project management tools have been developed over the years that allow leaders to monitor and adjust team behavior as events progress toward a completed project. Unfortunately, almost all of these traditional management measures are historical in nature." Mission statement of "Process Metrics," University Research Institute, Houston, Tex.

84   A reference to "Berlin Air," Paul Lincke's march of the same name and Berlin's unofficial anthem—not surprisingly, since there is such a "thing" as Berlin air, or vice versa, because of the march there is such a thing.

85   Hannah Arendt, *The Human Condition* (Chicago: University of Chicago Press, 1958). A proposition that by turning our relation into a pollical question, that once we engage the world of things we have to accept them as citizens in need of spokes-persons (Latour).

86   Giorgio Agamben, *The Signature of All Things: On Method* (New York: Zone Books, 2009), 33–80.

87   My friend Roemer van Thorn made me aware of "the gentleness of the objects," and I realized that I have stumbled on my own petard by not listening to the things-in-making. What is known as *media constraint* has an opposite side that we often ignore: *the object's agency.*

88   Samuel Beckett, *Watt* (London: Calder Jupiter Books, 1963), 133.

89   Teaching with Wolf D. Prix at Sci-Arc in the 1980s, we ask the students to design buildings that move: the final results are cabooses on long legs, stumbling around the studio floor.

90   Gökhan Kovalek, "Spinoza and Architecture: The Air of the Future," *Log* 49 (Summer 2020), 116. Kovalek's important work on Spinoza is, like *Blu*, a latecomer to my work, inserted here as a marker for any future work I do on objects. The remainder of the chapter is not a reflection of Spinoza's thinking but of "collusion" as its prefiguration.

91   Michel Foucault, *The Order of Things: An Archeology of the Human Sciences* (New York: Vintage, 1994), 387.

92   Agamben, *The Signature of All Things*, trans. L. D'Isanto with Kevin Attell (New York: Zone Books, 2009), 35.

93   Michel Serres, The Parasite (Minneapolis: University of Minnesota Press, 2007), 225–26. "The laws are written for it, defined relative to it, and we bend to these laws. [In fact,] the ball isn't there for the body; the exact contrary is true: the body is the object of the ball; playing is nothing else but making oneself the attribute of the ball as a substance."

94   The absence of a corridor serving and separating the rooms in the four-clover plan is a gift to my conception of the Empty Plan—a plan without instructions. A plan given to aesthetics—to our senses. As Robert Evans suggests, the corridor, in its puritan conception, is there to separate the sexes, providing privacy and "the removal of potential sources of irritation." Originally, it is the way to separate the servants from ladies and gentlemen. The corridor is thus the emblem of segregation. Robert Evans, Figures, Doors, and Passages (London: Architectural Association, 1997), 70–80.

95   See Roemer van Toorn's post on The Quasi-Object at https://www.roemervantoorn.nl/quasiobject.html

96   Bruno Latour, We Have Never Been Modern, trans. Catherine Porter (Cambridge, Mass.: Harvard University Press, 1993), 55. My understanding of this complex suggestion is that known objects are known because inseparable from the social milieu they exist in, and therefore fabricated by that same milieu; in addition shared and fabricated by many. Consequently, not "just hard parts of naturel" but alive, living among us. I see this bondage to objects as an opportunity to erase the 'just' and simultaneously open the door on the 'hard.'

97   Susan Sontag, "Against Interpretation," in Against Interpretation and Other Essays (New York: Picador, 1964), 10.

98   A schematic drawing of an object with short legs titled Dummy w/ Two Very Short Legs or Spurs and dated 2.17.1992 appears in Per Kirkeby's Natural History and Evolution. The book has text on one page and a facing blank page. My three-year old son begins drawing on one of the blank pages and I continue; during this time a series objects begins wandering outside the earlier generation. A series of molds appears, all imprints of actual objects. These outsiders are all useless—unless you feel furniture needs a coat in the chilly Alps.

99   Edward Dimendberg, Excluded Middle: Toward a Reflective Architecture and Urbanism (Houston: Rice School of Architecture; San Francisco: William Stout Architectural Books, 2002).

100   John Irving, Setting Free the Bears (New York: Random House, 1968).

Lars Lerup

Acquisitions Editor: David Marold, Birkhäuser Verlag, A-Vienna
Content & Production Editor: Bettina R. Algieri, Birkhäuser Verlag, A-Vienna
Proofreading: Sue Pickett
Cover design: Floyd Schulze
Layout and typography: Ekke Wolf, A-Vienna
Image editing: Pixelstorm, A-Vienna
Printing: Holzhausen, die Buchmarke der Gerin Druck GmbH, A-Wolkersdorf
Paper: Munken print white 15, 100 g
Typeface: Utopia, Futura Now

All images, unless stated otherwise: Lars Lerup

Library of Congress Control Number: 2021948987

Bibliographic information published by the German National Library
The German National Library lists this publication in the Deutsche
Nationalbibliografie; detailed bibliographic data are available on the
Internet at http://dnb.dnb.de.

ISBN 978-3-0356-2510-3
e-ISBN (PDF) 978-3-0356-2511-0

© 2022 Birkhäuser Verlag GmbH, Basel
P.O. Box 44, 4009 Basel, Switzerland
Part of Walter de Gruyter GmbH, Berlin/Boston

9 8 7 6 5 4 3 2 1   www.birkhauser.com